Tips for Singers

Performing, Auditioning, and Rehearsing

by Carolyn Wilkins

Edited by Jonathan Feist

Berklee Press

Vice President: Dave Kusek
Dean of Continuing Education: Debbie Cavalier
Chief Operating Officer: Robert F. Green
Managing Editor: Jonathan Feist
Editorial Assistants: Emily Goldstein, Rajasri Millikarjuna, Jonathan Whalen
Cover Designer: Robert Heath

ISBN 978-0-87639-089-4

DISTRIBUTED BY

HAL•LEONARD®
CORPORATION

1140 Boylston Street
Boston, MA 02215-3693 USA
(617) 747-2146

Visit Berklee Press Online at
www.berkleepress.com

7777 W. BLUEMOUND RD. P.O. BOX 13819
MILWAUKEE, WISCONSIN 53213

Visit Hal Leonard Online at
www.halleonard.com

CONTENTS

CD TRACKS

Carolyn Wilkins, Piano, Keyboards, and Vocals
Carrie Jahde, Drums
Shu Odamura, Guitar
John Voigt, Bass
Peter Kontrimas, Recording Engineer, PBS Studios, Westwood, MA

1. Introduction
2. Rhythm Reading Examples
3. Guitar Power Chords
4. Common Chords in C
5. Vamp
6. "Swing Low, Sweet Chariot" Arrangement
7. Practicing "Swing Low, Sweet Chariot"
8. "Stand Up" Piano/Vocal Arrangement
9. "Stand Up" Band Arrangement
10. "Stand Up" Groove Demo: Rock
11. "Stand Up" Groove Demo: Blues Shuffle
12. "Stand Up" Groove Demo: Reggae
13. "Stand Up" Groove Demo: Swing
14. "Stand Up" Groove Demo: Bossa
15. Drum Set Demo
16. Rhythm Section Function Demo: Pop Ballad
17. Rhythm Section Function Demo: Swing
18. Poor Writing for Background Vocals
19. Better Writing for Background Vocals

ACKNOWLEDGMENTS

This book is dedicated to:

The Light within each of us—let it shine, shine, shine!

All my ancestors. Without their steady perseverance in the face of insurmountable odds, I would not be standing here today. Ibaye!

My father Julian Wilkins, who taught me how to write, and my mother, Elizabeth Wilkins, who taught me how to sing.

My husband John Voigt for his endless patience, enduring love, and creative energy.

My heartfelt thanks goes out to my editor Jonathan Feist and my contributors Greg Badolato, Walter Beasley, Armsted Christian, Gabrielle Goodman, Renese King, Nancy Morris, Diane Richardson, Jan Shapiro, Jetro da Silva, Lisa Thorson, Rob Rose, Ann Marie Wilkins, and Ken Zambello. This book could not have been written without their expertise, patience, and insightful advice.

PREFACE

The hall is filled to capacity. The audience buzzes expectantly as they wait for the performance to begin. The lights dim and the curtain rises, revealing a small group of musicians poised at their instruments. Taking a deep breath, the star of the show adjusts her hair one more time, smoothes her dress, and steps into the spotlight. Acknowledging the applause of her fans with a smile, she nods confidently to the band, and the music begins.

Later, after a standing ovation and five encores, friends and admirers gather outside the star's dressing room offering compliments and flowers. "Miss Jones!" a reporter yells out from the crowd. "Can you tell our readers the secret of your overnight success?"

Perhaps in your fantasy, you are rocking a stadium full of fans screaming along to your latest megahit. Or you are backstage at the Apollo hanging out with Mary J. Blige, Stevie Wonder, and India Arie. Maybe you are stepping out of your stretch limo on the way to the Grammys, or signing autographs for fans outside a stage door on Broadway.

Whatever your fantasy, the reporter's question about the secret of your success is always the same. And so is the answer. No success, no matter how apparently "meteoric," ever happens overnight.

Time and time again, the biographies of great performers in every genre reveal that "sudden" success comes only after a long period of dedicated study away from the limelight.

Hopefully, you have already enlisted your most important ally in your quest for success. This vital ally is, of course, your voice teacher. If you don't yet have a voice teacher, the best way to begin your search is by contacting the teachers at your local high school, college, or community music school. If a local college has a music major, they may well have faculty or high level graduate students who teach privately. Another good reference is the National Association of Teachers of Singing, www.NATS.org. Their Web site contains a database that can link you to voice teachers all over the world. Whether you are planning to perform on a Broadway stage, in a hip-hop club, in a rock stadium, or in your own living room, your voice is your most valuable asset. Learning to train and care for it properly is an enormously worthwhile investment.

In today's competitive market, however, it takes more than a well-trained voice to have a lasting career in the music business. This book will address the many critical skills that, in addition to vocal technique, are essential to becoming a successful professional musician, such as how to choose songs that are right for you, how to practice/arrange/rehearse with a band, how to be your best on stage, how to publicize your event, and so much more.

Each chapter focuses on a particular aspect of music performance. Some chapters may be more applicable to your particular situation than others. If you find the information in a particular chapter doesn't seem relevant, feel free to skip over that section. If you want to study an area in more depth, I have included a list of resource materials at the end of this book.

Chinese philosopher Lao Tse once said, "A journey of ten thousand miles begins with one step." I invite you to take your first step with me into the world of successful vocal performance.

PART I

Performance

CHAPTER 1

Choosing Songs

Whitney Houston has long been one of my favorite singers. I just love the sweeping majesty of her range and the power she brings to the climaxes of her songs. When I was first learning to sing, I would buy the sheet music for each new song she recorded and try to copy every nuance. If the song went up too high for me, I would move it to a lower key. If the song went too low, I would raise it (see chapter 3). If the pacing of the song didn't work for me, I would try speeding it up or slowing it down. But no matter what I did, I was never able to get that soaring quality that Whitney achieved so effortlessly.

In twenty years of teaching, I have heard many talented students perform Whitney's songs. But rarely have I heard them sung in a way that moved me as much as the original performance. Obviously, Whitney Houston is a wonderful vocalist who would probably sound great singing "Mary Had a Little Lamb." But there is another factor at work here: All of Houston's hit songs were selected with her specific voice in mind. Then, every aspect of the songs (key, arrangement, tempo, and mood) was hand tailored to highlight Whitney's vocal strengths and minimize her vocal weaknesses.

Most of us do not have the luxury of a team of talented producers and songwriters at our disposal. But nonetheless, the principle remains the same. When choosing a song, look for one that best complements your unique vocal skill set. Here are three major factors you should consider:

1. Style/Attitude/Lyrics
2. Range
3. Register

STYLE/ATTITUDE/LYRICS

The primary purpose of performing is not to sing a pretty melody or show what a nice voice you have. The primary reason for the existence of any song is to communicate a message to the audience. What is the style and attitude of the song? What are the lyrics about? Is this a message that you truly feel comfortable with and can convey confidently?

For example, if you are singing a song about the ecstasies of physical love but are embarrassed at the thought of sharing these feelings before a crowd of strangers, your song—no matter how well sung—will fall flat.

If you are singing a song about how badly you want to hurt your two-timing lover when deep down you can't really imagine anyone having such extreme feelings, your song will fall flat once again.

Does this mean you need to have shot someone, come through a heroin addiction, or experienced a major life catastrophe in order to give a convincing performance? I don't think so. If that were the case, most professional singers would have to step off the stage.

The fact is that each of us has a full range of complex emotions bottled up within us, from the most lethal rage to the heights of ecstatic bliss. When choosing a song, we as performers must be willing to tap into these hidden wells of emotional energy. In order to convince our audience that what we are singing about is real, our vocal timbre, body language, articulation of lyrics, range, and register must be 100 percent consistent with the message of the song.

There are many songs that I adore when performed by someone else but cannot identify with enough emotionally to perform well. Before making the final selection of songs I am considering for a performance, I will often do a dramatic reading of the lyrics for a family member or close friend. If I feel extreme discomfort or awkwardness in doing this, it may be that this song is not one that I can do effectively.

Performing a song will make you plumb the depths of your inner being. For those few moments that you are singing it, you become the message. So be careful what you sing about, and make sure that you are comfortable with and capable of conveying its message effectively.

RANGE

The *range* of a song is the distance from its lowest note to its highest note, including any riffs or embellishments you may choose to add to its original melody.

Many popular songs are written within a range of an octave or an octave and a half—a distance of eight to twelve white notes on the piano keyboard. Songs that have a range wider than two octaves (sixteen white notes on the piano keyboard) can be quite challenging to sing.

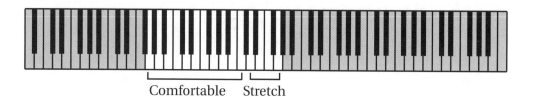

Comfortable   Stretch

Fig. 1.1. Vocal Song Range on Keyboard

It is possible to move the whole tonal center of the song up or down a few steps (see chapter 3), but if the range of the song is extremely wide, chances are that some of it will fall into a difficult register for your voice.

REGISTER

The human voice comes in six different basic voice types: soprano, mezzo-soprano, alto, tenor, baritone, and bass. Each one of these types has a different range:

Bass

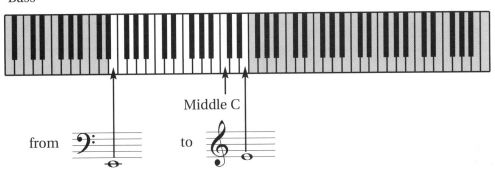

Baritone

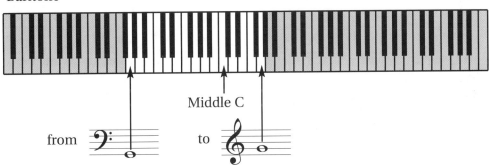

Tenor

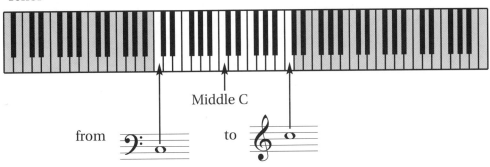

Alto (Contralto)

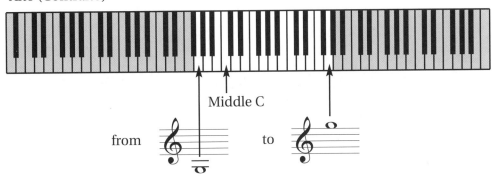

Mezzo-Soprano

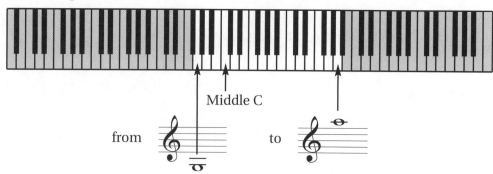

Soprano

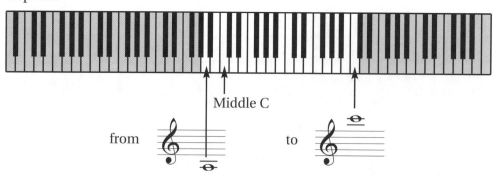

Fig. 1.2. Vocal Ranges

It's important to remember, however, that each voice is unique and these ranges are only generic estimates. This is particularly true for younger singers whose voices have not fully matured. Working with a good voice teacher can help you to discover your true vocal range, which may be far more expansive than you imagined.

The *register* of a song refers to the part of the voice in which it is sung. The lower register, commonly called the "chest voice," extends from your lowest notes through the middle of your range. This register is characterized by a thick, rich tone color (think later Sarah Vaughan or Isaac Hayes). When pushed to the outer limits of its range or volume, the chest voice gives us that commanding and forceful tone commonly referred to as "belting." Common examples of this style are Whitney Houston at the climax of one of her great power ballads ("I Will Always Love You," for example) or the alto section in a good "shout down the church" gospel choir.

The upper register in the voice is referred to as the "head voice." It extends from around the middle of your voice to the top of where you can comfortably sing. The sound of the head voice can range from the light, bell-like tones of early Joni Mitchell to the soaring soul vibrato of a Patti LaBelle. Opera singers do most of their singing in head voice, while many great pop stars have built entire careers while staying in the chest register.

Men also have a "falsetto register," which is located above their head voice. This voice is very light, almost ethereal in nature and should not be pushed or belted. This register has seduced women around the globe when used by such masters as D'Angelo, Marvin Gaye, and Smokey Robinson. Most of us have an area of six or seven notes in the middle of the range that can be sung in either head or chest voice. Your ability to choose the best register (head, chest, or a mixture of both) in which you sing a song will have a profound impact on how it is perceived by your audience.

For just a moment, try singing a few notes in the middle of your range first in chest voice and then in head voice. Notice how different they sound. Where does the song that you are considering lie in your range? Would you be singing it mostly in head voice or in chest voice?

Does the song have a wide range that would span both the head and chest voices? If so, would you need to move smoothly between the two registers? This is often the case when singing jazz standards. If you listen to jazz singers such as Diane Reeves or Ella Fitzgerald, there is a consistent sound from the top to the bottom of their ranges. Unless you listen very closely, you will not be able to tell when or how these artists transition from the head to the chest voice in the course of a song.

Or, does the song require different vocal colors to predominate in different sections? Are there some sections that you would want to sing in sweet head tones, while others might be sung with more of a belting sound?

Each register of your voice has a special inherent quality that can be very effective in getting your message across. Generally speaking, the chest voice is great for making strong, assertive statements, while the head is more sweet, airy, and ethereal. There are hundreds of ways to blend and play with combining these timbres. This is part of the great joy of singing. No two voices ever sound exactly alike, and there are an infinite number of ways to interpret any song. The important thing is to make sure that the qualities required by the song you perform are vocal qualities that you can in fact carry off with confidence.

Does your song require a deep, rich chest voice to be effective? If you are just starting out on your vocal journey and have not yet developed this end of your instrument, raising the tonal center of the song to put more of it in your head voice may be a solution. Or it may be that after you try this, the song loses its warmth and power. If this is the case, it may be that this particular song is not for you.

Conversely, does that song you have chosen require a high B♭? As much as I love drama, I would not recommend the drama involved in wondering if you will be able to hit the high note at the climax of the song every time you get up to perform. If you have not spent a lot of time working on your head tones, this song may not be for you. Once again, it may be that by lowering the key, you can bring the high notes within range. But if after you lower the key, the song loses its brightness and shimmer, then regretfully, you may have to let it go.

CHAPTER 2

Reading Music Notation

Expectations for vocalists today are higher than ever before. Increasing numbers of singers are receiving professional training, either on their own or at a music school. Your competition is coming into the job market vocally skilled, musically literate, and knowledgeable about all aspects of the music business. If you are unable to read music, you are putting yourself at a significant disadvantage.

Maybe you think that your manager, piano player, arranger, or significant other is going to cover this area—learning the songs, teaching them to you, writing the charts, rehearsing the band, etc. But stop for a moment and ask yourself one very important question. Do you really want to be *totally* dependent on someone else to handle this vital aspect of your career? What if you have a falling out with this indispensable soul the night before the gig?

Am I saying that you can't have a musical director who will help lift your performance to the next level? Of course not. But if you are musically literate, you will be able to evaluate and respond to your music director's suggestions from a place of knowledge.

The ability to read and write music is one of the most important skills that any professional vocalist can acquire. It enables you to work in a confident and independent manner, no matter what the musical setting. Knowledge is power, so let's get started.

Anyway, it's not as hard as you think.

THE ELEMENTS OF MUSIC

Music can be divided into three basic elements: pitch (the twelve distinct sounds that make up our tonal palette), rhythm, and harmony. As vocalists, our first concern is to be able to read, write, and sing melodies. A melody is nothing more than a series of pitches strung together in a particular rhythm. Let's start by getting a better understanding of how the twelve pitches are written.

Pitch

The grand staff (see below) is a visual representation of the most commonly used pitches in music ranging from the lowest to the highest. There are further pitches at each end of the spectrum, but they are rarely used in popular music. The grand staff is composed of two separate ranges, or clefs. The upper range, designated by the treble clef (𝄞), generally covers the pitches from middle C on the piano on up. The lower range, designated by the bass clef (𝄢), generally covers the pitches from middle C on down.

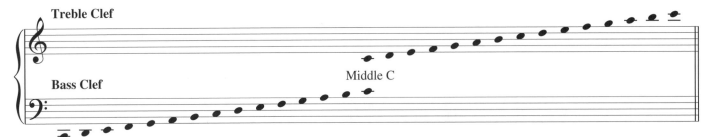

Fig. 2.1. Grand Staff

Each pitch is given a letter name from A through G. After G, the sequence begins all over again on A. If you go to an acoustic piano (synthesizers and electric pianos have fewer notes and are therefore configured somewhat differently) and start on the farthest white key to the left, this is A. Each successive white key is the next letter of the alphabet until you get to G. The next white note will be A again, and you can clearly hear that this is the same pitch as the first A but higher. This relationship between one note and the same pitch eight white notes higher is known in music parlance as an "octave."

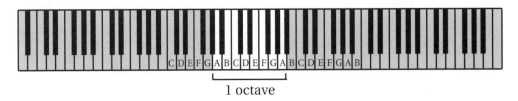

Fig. 2.2. One Octave (A to A)

The black keys on the piano give us the ability to raise or lower the pitch of the white keys by a half step. The half step is the smallest interval used in Western music between two notes. Any distance smaller than that will be perceived by the Western ear as being out of tune.

When we raise a note by a half step, this is referred to as "sharping" the note. If we raise the note A by a half step, for example, we refer to the new note as A-sharp. If we lower the pitch of any white note by a half step, we call this "flatting" the note. Flatting the note A would result in A-flat (A♭).

Fig. 2.3. A, A♯, A♭

The distance between a pair of notes separated by two half steps—the distance between C and D or A♭ and A♯, for example—is known as a "whole step."

Fig. 2.4. Whole Steps C to D and A♭ to A♯

Using half steps and whole steps as our musical "ruler," we can measure the distance between any two notes on the staff. Figure 2.5 shows an example of how C to E♭ can be described as 3 half steps.

Fig. 2.5. C to E♭: 3 Half Steps

The distance from G♯ to the next highest G♯ is 11 half steps or 5 1/2 whole steps.

Fig. 2.6. G♯ to G♮: 5 Half Steps

There is far more to be learned about how to notate musical pitches, but these essentials are enough to get you started. After reading just these few pages, you know how to locate any musical pitch on the grand staff. You are on your way to becoming a music reader!

Rhythm

Musical rhythm is composed of two basic elements: pulse and duration. Pulse is the constant and regular passage of musical time. The steady ticking of a clock, a metronome, or the rhythm of your heartbeat are all examples of the element of pulse in daily life.

Most music is built around a regularly recurring series of pulses. A marching army, for example (HUP, 2, 3, 4!) makes a clear pattern of four pulses in a repeating sequence. This sequence is known in musical terms as a "measure" and is designated in written music by a "bar line."

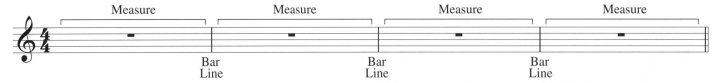

Fig. 2.7. Measures and Bar Lines

A note's duration indicates how long it is to be held relative to the music's pulse. Note durations are specified by noteheads, stems, and flags (or beams). Each different kind of note tells us something about its duration relative to other kinds of notes. In figure 2.8, each note is twice as long as its neighbor to the right.

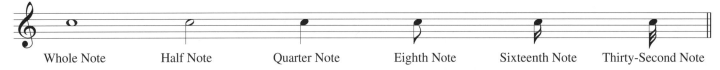

Fig. 2.8. Note Durations

Just as each kind of note is designed to last for a specific period of time relative to the basic pulse of the music, periods of silence, called "rests" in musical terminology, can also be indicated. Once again, each rest would last twice as long as its neighbor to the right.

Fig 2.9. Rests

A dot placed after a note or rest adds an extra half of the note's original value:

Fig 2.10. Dotted Notes and Rests

At the beginning of each piece of music, you will notice three symbols: first, the clef in which the music is written; second, the key signature, which designates the tonal center of the piece; and last, the time signature.

Fig. 2.11. Clef, Key Signature, and Time Signature

The two numbers in the time signature are written like a fraction. In 4/4 time, the top number indicates the number of pulses or "beats" per measure, while the bottom number indicates the kind of note that will receive one beat. In 4/4, the quarter note gets the beat and there are four of them in every measure.

In 3/4 time, there are three beats in every measure, and the quarter note receives one beat. In 6/8 time, there are six beats per measure, and the eighth note receives one beat.

How does this abstract concept translate in our everyday musical experience? Here are the time signatures of some well-known songs. If you pat your foot and whistle a few bars, you will begin to get a sense of how each grouping of pulses differs from the next.

2/4   Sousa, "The Stars and Stripes Forever"
3/4   Strauss, "On the Blue Danube"
4/4   "Swing Low, Sweet Chariot"
6/8   "Three Blind Mice"

Reading rhythms involves figuring out each note's duration relative to the underlying pulse.

Rhythms are notated in a very logical and mathematical fashion. In the following three rhythm reading examples, you have a pulse of four beats per measure underlying a written rhythm comprised of a combination of half notes, whole notes, quarter notes and eighth notes. While tapping your foot at a steady tempo and counting 1, 2, 3, 4 to indicate the pulse, clap your hands on the rhythms indicated. Try figuring out these rhythms, and then check yourself against the CD.

TRACK 2

Fig. 2.12. Rhythm Reading Practice

There is far more to be learned about reading rhythms than can be addressed in this brief chapter. If you are serious about your music career, and especially if you are a songwriter, you will need to master this crucial art. For more information on reading and writing rhythms, please refer to the Resources section at the end of this book.

Key Signatures

Most music is built around a home base—the note to which all other notes in the song resolve. This note is called the song's tonal center, or "tonic." Imagine singing "Twinkle, Twinkle, Little Star" to your little nephew and changing the last note.

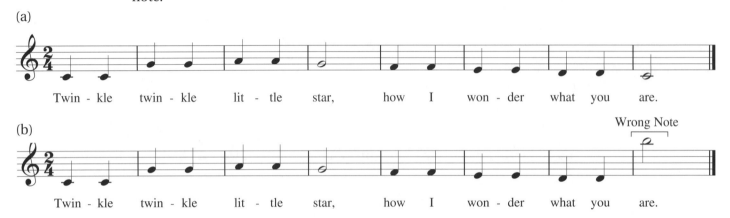

Fig. 2.13. "Twinkle, Twinkle, Little Star" (a) as Written (b) with Wrong Note

Your nephew would instantly know you sang a wrong note because your mistake involved the song's tonal center. This last note must be sung correctly for the song to make sense.

The purpose of the key signature is to indicate the tonal center or "key" of the piece. The key signature shows us this tonal center (also called the tonic note) by indicating the number of flats or sharps in its major scale. Remember Julie Andrews in *The Sound of Music*? "Do, a Deer," etc? She was teaching her students the major scale, using a common ear training system called solfege, which pairs words with notes based on a tonal center. A major scale consists of eight notes whose whole and half steps have a very specific relation to each other. If you go to the piano and play the eight notes from middle C to the next C, you will be playing a major scale.

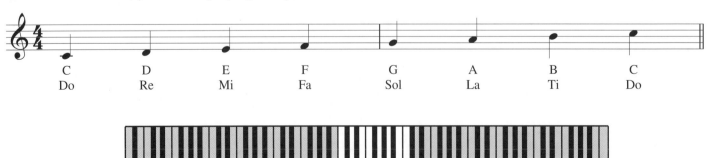

Fig. 2.14. C Major Scale

When reading a piece of music, the key signature is always taken into account. In the key of E, for example, there are four sharps: F, C, G, and D. This means that for the duration of the piece, these four notes will always be sharped unless preceded by a natural sign (♮) or the key signature changes. Figure 2.15 shows the key signatures for the major keys and their tonic notes.

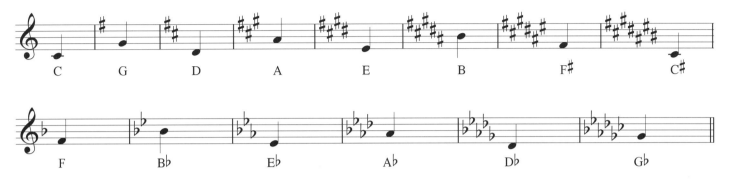

Fig. 2.15. Key Signatures

Chord Notation

The third major element of music is harmony: the sound created when multiple pitches occur at once. There are almost as many different ways to create musical harmony as there are ways to create music itself. In the world of popular music, the term "harmony" refers to the chords that support the melody of a song. Two-note chords are called "power chords," and they are very common in rock and pop music—particularly in guitar parts. Sometimes they also repeat the tonic note up an octave.

TRACK 3

Fig 2.16. C Power Chord

The chart below shows you the notes that make up the most common kinds of chords and the symbols most often used to abbreviate them. All these chords are written with C as the root, but of course, in real music they could be transposed to start on any pitch.

TRACK 4

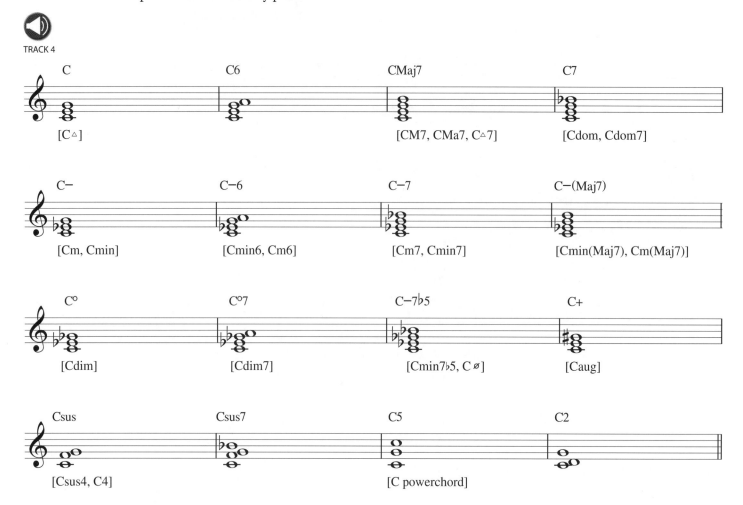

Fig. 2.17. Common Chords in C

This has been a brief overview of how music is notated. You now know the names of the two most commonly used clefs, the names of the musical notes, and how to raise or lower them. You have also learned about the most common kinds of rhythm and chord notation and what key and time signatures are used for. Congratulations! You have now made a major step on your journey to musical literacy, and I urge you to develop it as much as you can. In the next chapter, we will put your newfound knowledge to work selecting the proper key for your song.

CHAPTER 3

Finding Your Key and Transposing

How many times have you heard a singer grasping desperately for notes that were clearly out of his or her range? Now that you have armed yourself with a little knowledge about the basics of music notation, this embarrassing situation need never happen to you. There is no need to sing songs that are too high or too low for you just because that is the key in which their sheet music is written. In this chapter, I will show you an easy method of adjusting the tonal center of any song to the key that is best for your voice.

Remember the earlier section about key signatures? Every song has one. By changing the key, we change the song's tonal center.

You must find the key in which the whole song, from top to bottom, lies most comfortably in your voice. Suppose, for example, you were trying to learn to sing the chorus of the African-American spiritual, "Swing Low, Sweet Chariot" (generally attributed to Wallis Willis). Say that in your sheet music, the lowest note is C while the highest note is D an octave plus a whole step higher.

Suppose, however, that you are a low alto. For your voice, it would be best to have the lowest note be G below middle C, and the highest note the A an octave plus a whole step higher. So, here's what we've determined so far:

Original version of "Swing Low, Sweet Chariot":

Fig. 3.1. "Swing Low, Sweet Chariot" Range: Key of F

But for you, the ideal range of "Swing Low, Sweet Chariot" would be:

Fig. 3.2. Range G to A

How are we going to adjust the sheet music so that whoever's accompanying you will be able to play it in your key? Here's where your new knowledge of notation basics will come in handy.

In its original format, the tonal center or key for "Swing Low, Sweet Chariot" was F. How do we know that? By looking at the key signature: one flat. (When you explore music notation in more depth, you will learn that each key signature represents both a major and a minor key. But for the purposes of getting started on the basics of music notation, we will be addressing major keys only.) Incidentally, as is often the case, F is also the last note of the piece. Let's now look at the ideal lowest note of "Swing Low, Sweet Chariot." Referring back to the diagram shown above, we can see that your ideal lowest note would be low G, instead of middle C, as written in the original.

The next step is to determine the number of half steps between the original lowest note and your ideal lowest note. This is the number of half steps by which you must move all the notes of the song in order to notate it correctly in your new key. Let's take a look at what this process would look like:

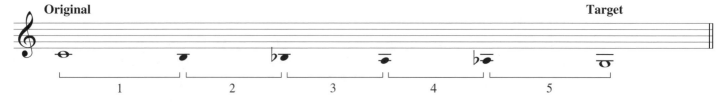

Fig. 3.3. Counting Half Steps from G to C

It's five half steps down, so we set all the notes of the song five half steps down. Here's the transposed version:

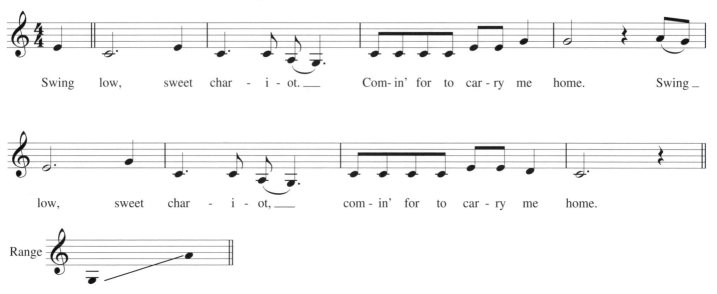

Fig. 3.4. "Swing Low, Sweet Chariot" Range: Key of C

Now, the song ends on the note C. This is your new tonal center. Checking back over your list of key signatures, you see that the key of C has no sharps or flats. You can also see that your new tonal center (C) is exactly the same number of half steps away from the old tonal center (F) as your new lowest note is from your old lowest note. Voila! You have now successfully transposed this song.

Once you master this method, it is surprisingly easy to use. Because it is an essentially mechanical process, computer notation programs can easily transpose sheet music to the key of your choice. One word of caution with computer transposition, however. Because computer transposition is automated, mistakes are common, particularly when it comes to the *enharmonic spellings* of notes.

ENHARMONIC SPELLINGS

What are enharmonic spellings? Let's return to our trusty keyboard graphic for a minute. If you take a look, you will see that raising A by a half step gives you the note A♯. Lowering the note B a half step gives you the note B♭. It doesn't take a rocket scientist to figure out that—egad!—A♯ and B♭ are two different names for the same note! How will you know which name to use?

A♯/B♭

Fig 3.5. Piano Keyboard Showing A♯/B♭

The best way to determine between two enharmonic spellings is to look at the musical context of the note in question. If the note is part of a descending passage, then since flats are used for lowering the pitch of notes, it is probably best to call it B♭. If the note is in an ascending musical passage, then since sharps are used for raising the pitch of notes, it probably would be best to call it A♯.

Fig. 3.6. Enharmonics and Melodic Direction

If the song's key signature is made up of flats and most of the other notes in the piece are flats, then B♭ will be the most easily understood spelling. The converse is true if the song is written in a sharp key signature.

One last amazing thing: If you take a close look at our piano keyboard, you will see that "sharping" the note B gives us C on the keyboard. Similarly, sharping the note E gives us F. Unless there is a pressing musical reason for writing B♯ or E♯ (take a look at the key signature for C♯ major, for example), it is best to write F instead of E♯ and C instead of B♯.

The chart below will help you find the correct distance in half steps between any two notes. It also lists the enharmonic spellings for each note. To use it, simply find the original pitch on the horizontal axis of the chart. On the vertical axis of the chart, count up by the number of half steps desired, and you will find the correct transposed pitch.

Transposition Chart

Whole Steps	Half Steps													
5½	11	C♭/B	C/B♯	D♭/C♯	D	E♭/D♯	E	F/E♯	G♭/F♯	G	A♭/G♯	A	B♭/A♯	B
5	10	B♭/A♯	C♭/B	C/B♯	D♭/C♯	D	E♭/D♯	E	F/E♯	G♭/F♯	G	A♭/G♯	A	B♭/A♯
	9	A	B♭/A♯	C♭/B	C/B♯	D♭/C♯	D	E♭/D♯	E	F/E♯	G♭/F♯	G	A♭/G♯	A
4	8	A♭/G♯	A	B♭/A♯	C♭/B	C/B♯	D♭/C♯	D	E♭/D♯	E	F/E♯	G♭/F♯	G	A♭/G♯
	7	G	A♭/G♯	A	B♭/A♯	C♭/B	C/B♯	D♭/C♯	D	E♭/D♯	E	F/E♯	G♭/F♯	G
3	6	G♭/F♯	G	A♭/G♯	A	B♭/A♯	C♭/B	C/B♯	D♭/C♯	D	E♭/D♯	E	F/E♯	G♭/F♯
	5	F/E♯	G♭/F♯	G	A♭/G♯	A	B♭/A♯	C♭/B	C/B♯	D♭/C♯	D	E♭/D♯	E	F/E♯
2	4	E	E♯/F	G♭/F♯	G	A♭/G♯	A	B♭/A♯	C♭/B	C/B♯	D♭/C♯	D	E♭/D♯	E
	3	E♭/D♯	E	F/E♯	G♭/F♯	G	A♭/G♯	A	B♭/A♯	C♭/B	C/B♯	D♭/C♯	D	E♭/D♯
1	2	D	E♭/D♯	E	F/E♯	G♭/F♯	G	A♭/G♯	A	B♭/A♯	C♭/B	C/B♯	D♭/C♯	D
	1	D♭/C♯	D	E♭/D♯	E	F/E♯	G♭/F♯	G	A♭/G♯	A	B♭/A♯	C♭/B	C/B♯	D♭/C♯
		C/B♯	D♭/C♯	D	E♭/D♯	E	F/E♯	G♭/F♯	G	A♭/G♯	A	B♭/A♯	C♭/B	C/B♯
Half Steps			1	2	3	4	5	6	7	8	9	10	11	12
Whole Steps				1		2		3		4		5		6

Fig. 3.7. Transposition Chart

CHAPTER 4

More Notation:
Dynamics and Repeats

DYNAMICS

Much of our notation system is derived from the Italian language. To indicate the volume level (also known in music parlance as dynamics) of a particular section of music, abbreviations of Italian words are used:

Pianissimo	*pp*	Very soft
Piano	*p*	Soft
Mezzoforte	*mf*	Medium loud
Forte	*f*	Loud
Fortissimo	*ff*	Very loud

If you want to gradually increase the volume of the music over a number of measures, you write the sign ⟨ or the Italian word "crescendo" ("cresc." for short).

If you want to gradually decrease the volume of the music over a number of measures, you write the sign ⟩ or the Italian word "decrescendo" ("decresc." for short).

REPEATS

In order to avoid writing out reams of additional pages, musicians over the years have created some simple music-reading shortcuts. Here are the most common ones:

Repeat Sign

Fig. 4.1. Repeat Sign

Any music contained within these two signs must be played twice. To repeat something more than twice, you must indicate either the specific number of times the passage will be repeated or place the words "repeat and fade" or "vamp." The term "vamp" indicates that the phrase in question should be repeated over and over again. For example, your accompanist might "vamp" a section of music as an introduction until you are ready to begin singing.

TRACK 5

Fig. 4.2. Vamp

Whoever is reading this will know that they are to repeat the section in question over and over until you cue them to either stop or go on to the next section.

First and Second Endings

Fig. 4.3. First and Second Ending

When the repeated section is played the first time, the first ending (1.) is played. On the second time through, the second ending (2.) is played. More complex songs may have three or more different endings for a repeated section, but the principle involved is the same.

Coda

A coda ( ) is a separate section that usually (but not always) contains the end of the song. It is set apart from the rest of the music by its special sign in two places. The first time you see the coda sign, you must jump to the coda section. The next time you see the coda sign will indicate the location of the coda section. Coda is Italian for "end" or "tail."

D.C.

When you see *D.C.*, return to the beginning of the song. *D.C.* is an abbreviation for the Italian words "Da Capo," which means to go back to the beginning.

D.C. al Fine

Go back to the beginning and play until you see the *Fine* symbol. *Fine* is Italian for "the end."

D.C. al Coda

Go back to the beginning, and proceed to the first coda symbol (⊕). From the first coda symbol, jump to the coda section of the music to finish the song.

D.S.

The *D.S.* marker means return to the place in the music indicated by the sign (𝄋). *D.S.* is Italian for "Del Segno," or "from the sign." *D.S.* might also be followed with "al Fine" or "al Coda."

CHAPTER 5

Practicing Your Song

When I first began studying voice, I used to practice an hour a day faithfully before breakfast every morning. Much of this practice time was devoted to singing my piece over and over from beginning to end. I would launch into the song and go until I made a mistake. Then, after a few choice curse words, I would start again, vowing to sing it correctly the next time through. Instead, I would usually find myself repeating the same mistake with perhaps a few new wrong notes thrown in for good measure. Thoroughly irritated, I would doggedly return to the beginning and try to sing my song again. When I returned to the offending measure, I would sing it wrong yet again. I had an old teacher once that used to call this form of practice "perfecting your mistakes."

IDENTIFYING THE PROBLEM

In order to practice a piece of music effectively, you must break it down and analyze the cause of your mistakes. Is the problem with the pitch? Is the problem in the rhythm? Is pronouncing the words causing you to make a mistake? A thoughtful analysis of the problem will help you to avoid similar mistakes in the future.

Practicing the Melody

Have you ever heard someone singing along with their favorite song, thinking they were sounding great, only to be exposed as hopelessly off key the minute the CD was turned off? Learning the melody of a song pitch by pitch, away from the original recording, will help you distinguish fact from fantasy where your singing is concerned. If you can sing a song and sound great without accompaniment, then you know you have really got it.

Let's suppose you are trying to learn the classic African-American spiritual "Swing Low, Sweet Chariot."

Fig. 5.1. "Swing Low, Sweet Chariot" (Arrangement)

Let's say that you are having problems with the part of the song that goes, "Tell all of my friends I'm a-comin' too." Every time you try to sing this section, one note sounds horribly wrong. Rather than tearing your hair out, let's use an analytical approach to identify the source of the problem.

TRACK 7

To determine whether your mistake comes from an incorrect grasp of the melody, start at the beginning of the phrase, and sing the pitches without rhythm, using the syllable "ah." Singing the passage on "ah" out of rhythm and without lyrics will help you to focus on the flow of the melody. After you sing the passage through, be sure to check your pitch against the piano to make sure you are singing the notes correctly.

Written out, this exercise would look like this:

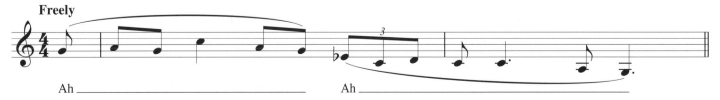

Fig. 5.2. "Swing Low" Pitch Exercise (Ah)

How did you do? If you breezed through the "problem" area using this method, go back and try to sing the passage in rhythm with lyrics. If you are now able to sing it to your satisfaction, then you may have cured this particular mistake.

Practicing the Rhythm

If it still doesn't sound right when you sing the passage, analyze whether your problem might be one of rhythm. Counting 1, 2, 3, 4 out loud, try clapping the rhythm of the problem passage.

Fig. 5.3. "Swing Low, Sweet Chariot" Rhythm Exercise (Clap)

Do you know how the rhythm should go when it is stripped of its melody and lyrics? If not, you may be singing the rhythm of the song incorrectly. Maybe this is the cause of your mistake. Go back to the passage, and sing it slowly, mentally counting 1, 2, 3, 4 as you do. Make sure that its rhythm is the same as the rhythm you clapped when counting 1, 2, 3, 4 earlier. If you are sure you have the rhythm correct but the passage still sounds wrong, there is another area to investigate.

Practicing the Lyrics

Sometimes a passage will sound fine on "ah" but fall apart once the lyric is added. When this happens, I find it helpful to practice chanting the lyrics on a single note, keeping my tongue and jaw as relaxed as possible. This method forces me to take my breath into consideration. Do I have enough air to get through each phrase? Where are the logical places to take a breath? How can I preserve the message of the song and still have enough air to get through the phrase?

Fig. 5.4. "Swing Low, Sweet Chariot" Lyric Exercise (Chant)

Sometimes, the problem is not in articulating the lyrics, but in remembering them. I like to memorize lyrics by saying them as if I were speaking to a friend. Sometimes, I practice by saying them in different rhythms, as if they were a rap song, or as if they were one long run-on sentence.

One singer I know memorizes lyrics by writing them out ten times in a row from memory. If this works for you, go for it. Say your lyrics while you are washing the dishes, doing the laundry, or whatever. The more deeply you can imprint them into your brain, the better the odds are that they will appear in their proper form under the stress of an important performance.

Intonation Problems

What happens if you have worked on each element of your song individually and it still sounds off key? Here are three areas to troubleshoot when you are having intonation problems.

1. Inner Hearing

Sometimes, people sing out of tune because they do not have an image of the correct pitch in their mind's ear. Though they may have a rough idea of the shape of the phrase in question, their grasp of specific pitches is not sufficiently clear.

Inner Hearing Exercise

Sitting at a piano, play the note in question several times, allowing the tone to die away before you strike the key again. Then sing the note, easily, in an unforced manner. Don't add any dynamics or vocal expression. If the pitch is a high one *and* you can sing that note easily in tune when doing your regular vocal warm-ups, sing it an octave lower at first, to avoid tiring yourself. The purpose here is to clearly get the sound of the pitch in your inner ear.

Once you can sing the "problem note" successfully, try singing the passage starting a couple of notes before it in the same relaxed way, out of tempo. If you are able to sing this part of the passage, keep adding notes until you are able to sing all the notes in the phrase easily and effortlessly.

2. Unnecessary Physical Tension

Physical tension is another common cause of intonation problems. Practice the passage in question in front of a mirror. Do the cords on your neck stand out? Does your face twist into a grimace? Do your shoulders hunch up or your chin jut out? We often go out of tune in the sections where we are most emotionally invested in the song. Without being aware of it, we are tightening up physically and mentally.

If you are habitually tense, try doing some stretches or the warm-up routine in chapter 13 to begin your practice session. As you become more aware of your body, it will be easier to notice and eliminate intonation problems caused by physical tension.

3. Breath Management

As you sing the troublesome passage, monitor your breath. Do you find yourself squeezing out the tail end of the phrase on your last bit of air? Notes sung without full breath support have a tendency to be unstable. In the excitement of performance, it is easy to forget to support your tone fully, especially in long phrases. But if you consciously plan your breaths during practice time, you will be far more likely to stay on key in the concert.

BAND REHEARSAL READINESS CHECKLIST

When you sing for the first time with a band, the presence of other instruments will make even the most familiar piece sound different. If you are at all insecure about your song, you may become disconcerted and unable to effectively use your rehearsal time.

Before you schedule your first run-through with the band, ask yourself the following questions:

1. Am I totally comfortable with the message, intent, and attitude of my song?
2. Is my song transposed into the best possible key for me?
3. Have I mastered my song's melody, rhythm, and lyrics? Do I have it memorized?

If you can honestly answer yes to those key questions, the next step will be to create a lead sheet for your song.

CHAPTER 6

Creating a Lead Sheet

The term lead sheet, or "chart," is used by musicians to describe a specific format for writing out the music to a song. A good lead sheet gives your band members the essential information they need to create your accompaniment, while at the same time leaving room for them to improvise the details.

PIANO SHEET MUSIC

People often assume that a lead sheet is the same thing as the piano sheet music for your song. This is not true, as you will see from the example below.

Track 8 on the CD is a song that I wrote called "Stand Up," being performed straight from the piano sheet music, also called a piano/vocal score.

TRACK 8

This sheet music contains a line for the vocal melody and lyrics and a grand staff below with the written-out piano accompaniment. On some music sheets, there are also chord symbols written above each measure to indicate the song's basic harmonies.

Stand Up

Music and Lyrics by
Carolyn Wilkins

You sit a-lone in the cor-ner   Hang-ing back   from the pack

let-ting life   pass you by   As your friend I've got to   say just what I   see

You can't hide   from des-ti-ny ___   Your spir-it's made   to

soar up to the sky   It's time to spread your wings   It's time for you   to

Verse
Funk

fly!

Don't be a - fraid __   to give it ev - ery - thing ya got
Don't be a - fraid __   of step - pin' out __ on your own

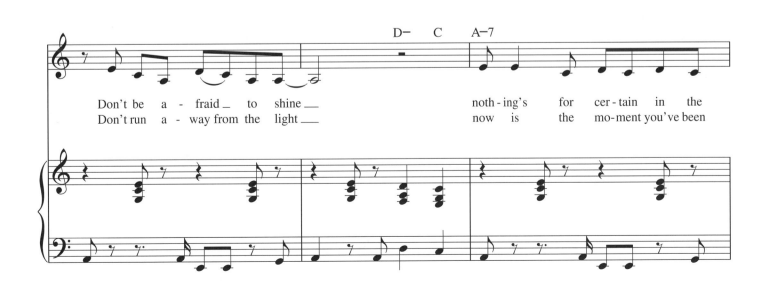

Don't be a - fraid __ to shine __   noth - ing's   for cer - tain in the
Don't run a - way from the light __   now is   the mo - ment you've been

Fig. 6.1. Piano/Vocal Score to "Stand Up"

This is all you need, if you are a songwriter trying to demo your song to recording artists or if you are planning to perform your song with only a piano player. But what happens if you want to sing your song with a band? A sheet music arrangement would be awkward and difficult for a band to read.

LEAD SHEETS

All the details of the accompaniment are spelled out in the piano score, but let's suppose you have in your group not only piano, but also bass, drums, and guitar. Should the bass player play the exact same notes as the piano's left hand? It would be a waste for the bass to merely replicate what the piano is already doing. Some of the bass notes written in the piano accompaniment are below the written range of the bass, in any case. What about the drums? What kind of beat should be played? When and where do you want to utilize the guitar? All of these questions can be resolved by creating a basic lead sheet.

A song's lead sheet has just a single-line melody, chord symbols, lyrics, and a few other directions. Musicians use this basic information to create parts that are appropriate for their instrument's role in the band—a different skill than just reading a completely written out part. All instruments can use the same lead sheet.

Let's hear the same song as played from the lead sheet shown below by an ensemble of piano, bass, drums, and guitar. Once your song is in a lead sheet format, it is much easier to customize and arrange it to fit your specific musical situation. In this instance, as recorded on track 9, I repeated part of the song to make room for a guitar solo over the bridge.

TRACK 9

Fig. 6.2. Standard Lead Sheet to "Stand Up"

This lead sheet provides musicians with the essential information they need to create an accompaniment for you, based on your own creative direction for the kind of arrangement you want to do. This lead sheet will be clearer and more convenient for your band to follow than the piano sheet music.

If you are a singer/songwriter and are attempting to notate your entire song from scratch, you will need to be able to accurately notate your song first before attempting to create a lead sheet. This process can take quite a bit of skill in music literacy. The resources in the appendix will help you write out your original songs.

Here's a step-by-step process for creating a lead sheet.

Step 1. Write Out the Melody

Your musicians need to be aware of what you're singing at all times in order to back you up in the best way possible. So, your first job is to copy out the melody.

Fig. 6.3. First Eight Bars of Melody

Step 2. Write Out the Lyrics

Set the lyrics under the melody. This way, your musicians are aware of everything you are doing and of the mood that your song is trying to convey.

Fig. 6.4. First Eight Bars of Melody with Lyrics

Step 3. Write the Chord Symbols above the Melody Line

Musicians usually do not need to know every detail of the written accompaniment to your song. They do need to know the basic chords that create its harmony, and when to change from chord to chord. When you write in the chord symbols, be sure to place them on the exact beat where you want the chord to change to avoid misunderstandings.

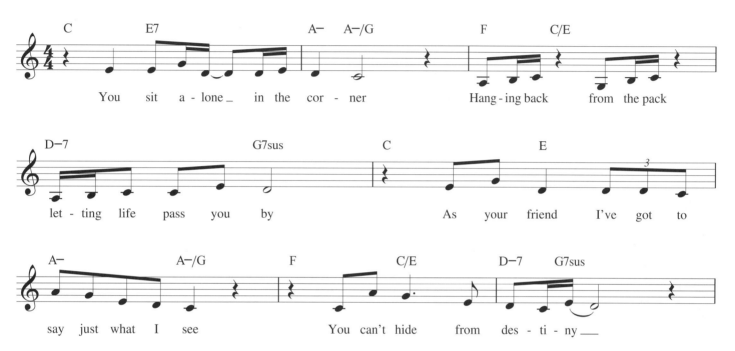

Fig. 6.5. First Eight Bars with Chord Symbols

Step 4. Label Song Sections Using Rehearsal Letters

When you're rehearsing with a group, it's handy to have indicators labeling each musical section. That way, if you need to stop and practice, say, the bridge of your song, the band will not have to have a lengthy discussion about where to find that section on your lead sheet. Rehearsal letters are also very helpful when musicians are sight-reading. If they get lost, they can clearly see where the next section of the music begins and thus get back on track.

Fig. 6.6. Rehearsal Letter A

Step 5. Indicate the Groove of the Song

Above the first measure, write the kind of groove in which the song is to be played. What do I mean by a groove? The groove is the repeating rhythm pattern, set up primarily by the bass and drums, that creates the "beat" of the song.

Each groove consists of a specific repeating rhythmic pattern. We all know this instinctively, if not in these exact terms. For example, you would definitely notice the difference if I played James Brown's "I Feel Good" as a waltz in 3/4 time rather than its normal sixties funk groove. Or if I sang "We Are the World" as a 1930s big-band swing tune instead of a pop ballad, as it is usually done.

The next few cuts on the CD illustrate how the A section of my song would sound played in a few of the most common grooves. Notice that with each of these grooves, the melody and the chords stay essentially the same. What changes is the way the band defines the rhythmic pulse. On the lead sheet, the only difference between styles is the groove indicated in the upper-left corner.

TRACK 10

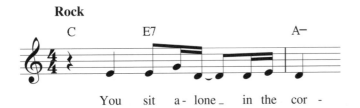
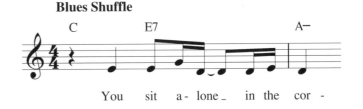

Fig. 6.7. Groove Indications: Rock and Funk

In order to interpret the melody and rhythms in accordance with each given style, you will need to develop a feel for what is "standard practice" in that style. Listen to the next four tracks on the CD and you will hear how I changed my interpretation of the melody to fit the designated groove.

At Berklee, we have a required course called *Rhythm Grooves* that teaches singers how to create lead sheets for their songs, and how to work in and identify different kinds of grooves. It is an exciting and challenging class, and believe me, you are a Wizard of Rhythm by the time you finish. But with what I have just showed you, you have enough information to get started.

You now have a basic lead sheet. This, coupled with clear verbal instructions from you and (if possible) a copy of the recording, should give your band all the information they need to play your song.

For more information about the finer points of lead-sheet writing and some excellent resource material to help you gain even greater proficiency, please look in the resources listed in the appendix.

CHAPTER 7

Hooking Up with the Rhythm Section: Roles and Functions in the Groove

Singing with a band is one of the most fun things you could ever imagine doing. But your first practice can be daunting if you do not understand the special dynamics involved in ensemble playing.

Each instrument in the band has a specific function that helps to create the total effect. The more fully you understand what each of them is trying to do, the better you will be able to communicate your musical vision for the piece. For years, singers were relentlessly patronized and undervalued by instrumental musicians because they were perceived as lacking the musical savvy to make intelligent judgments about their own accompaniments.

Sadly, many of us have relied in the past on musical "Svengalis"—piano players, musical directors, etc., to create our accompaniments for us. But now, armed with the knowledge you'll receive in this chapter, you will be able to clearly understand the role of each instrument in creating the total sound of the band.

DRUMS

The drummer is the keeper of the groove. Without a good beat, your music will not reach your audience with the desired impact. So how does the drummer do their thing?

TRACK 15

The basic drum kit is comprised of four basic elements:

1. Bass (Kick) Drum. The lowest sound in the drum kit, this instrument is played with a foot pedal. Often the bass drum will hook up with whatever rhythm the bass player is playing to create the fundamental groove of the song.

2. Snare Drum. The snare drum provides the accents that define the groove. In a pop or rock tune, the snare drum lays down the backbeat (beats 2 and 4 in 4/4 time) that gets the crowd up on their feet and clapping along.

3. Cymbals. Drummers use cymbals to create many kinds of musical colors and effects, but the two most basic cymbals used are the ride cymbal and the hi-hat. The hi-hat or "sock cymbal" is actually two cymbals that open and close to create a crisp sound. In swing grooves, this sound is often used to highlight the backbeat (beats 2 and 4 in 4/4 time). In many pop and funk grooves, the hi-hat is kept closed and provides the relentless pulse that makes this music danceable.

    The other commonly used cymbal is the ride cymbal, used to provide a consistent repeating pattern as a backdrop for the rest of the band.

4. Tom Toms. The basic drum kit has at least two tom toms, which are used to provide accents and vary the tonal color of the basic kit.

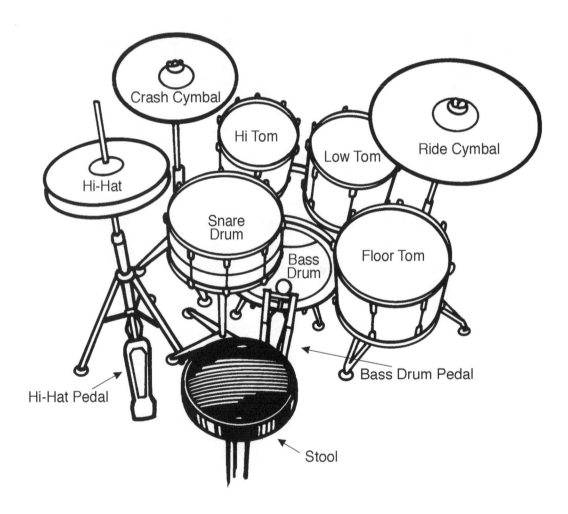

Fig. 7.1. Standard Drum Set

Once you understand what the drums are doing in a song, you will have a fair idea of how to make the whole band groove better.

BASS

It is the bass player's responsibility to create lines that lock in synch with the drummer. Without this, your band won't groove. At the same time, the bass is also responsible for playing the roots (the fundamental notes) of the song's chords.

KEYBOARD AND GUITAR

The piano and the guitar are responsible for filling out the harmony to your song. As we already learned, the bass player gives us the root or fundamental note of each chord. The piano and the rhythm guitar fill out these chords, putting your vocal melody in a harmonic context. In musician parlance, playing the chords that accompany another instrument is referred to as "comping."

Good musicians will complement and not overshadow you as you sing. Good comping will also contribute to the overall groove of the song—not too much, not too little. If you will be playing guitar or piano while you sing, the same advice applies. Sometimes, we are our own worst enemies when we accompany ourselves. Remember that it is your vocals that the audience will be listening for. Any accompaniment, no matter how beautiful, is a secondary priority.

TRACK 16

Let's listen now as the drums, bass, guitar, and piano play a basic pop ballad groove. Each part of the drum set enters separately, so that you can hear what each part of the kit adds to the overall sound. Also, notice how closely the bass part shadows the bass drum. If these two instruments are not in synch, your band will not have a danceable beat. Also notice how the piano and guitar are both playing the chords, but each instrument has its own comping pattern. This avoids unnecessary duplication (and therefore, muddying) of parts and makes the overall texture richer.

TRACK 17

Next, let's listen to the rhythm section play a swing groove. Notice how each instrument's part changes to accommodate this different rhythmic feel.

This style of bass playing is called "walking" bass in jazz lingo. Notice how important the bass player is to both the rhythm and the fundamental harmony of this song. Listen to how the guitar is playing four beats per measure all through this example. This is a common style for playing rhythm guitar on a swing tune.

The piano, bass, drums, and guitar comprise your band's "rhythm section." As we have seen, the rhythm section provides the basic groove and harmonic accompaniment that underlies your vocals. If you are on a limited budget, performing with just piano or guitar, bass, and drums will give you sufficient accompaniment to get the job done. But if you are able to add even one more instrument to your band, you can enhance the group's overall sound tremendously.

SOLO INSTRUMENTS

Solo instruments change the listener's focus of attention and thus vary the pace and texture of the song. A brief instrumental solo in the context of a pop tune can set up the dramatic final chorus or provide the wind down of energy needed to smooth the final fade.

In a rock or blues band, the lead guitar solo can become the main focus of the tune, raising the audience's energy and excitement level for several minutes before the vocals resume. The whole style of mainstream jazz depends on solos—lots of them, with instrument after instrument taking turns improvising over the tune's underlying harmony (called "chord changes," in jazz parlance).

As a vocalist, there is one cardinal rule to be aware of when using soloists. No one—but *no one*—in the band should be allowed to overpower the lead vocalist at any time, ever. Sometimes, an arrangement may call for a horn or guitar to play a countermelody or line under your voice. Always remember that no matter what else is going on at the time, the melody and the lyrics are the most important elements in the music. Nothing else should be allowed to take center stage while you are singing them. Can solo instruments be in dialogue with the lead vocals? Certainly. But just as in conversation, good dialogue is created by *listening* as much as by speaking.

CHAPTER 8

Arranging

The process of "arranging" involves embellishing the basic structure of a song in order to enhance its presentation. Background vocalists, extra instruments, or even extra musical sections may be added. In this chapter, we will talk about some arranging techniques that you can use to make your song sound more polished and professional.

BACKGROUND VOCALISTS

Background vocalists add a tremendous amount to an arrangement. Not only do they bring extra energy and visual interest, but they also add the elements of harmony and repetition to your performance. When auditioning background vocalists, here are some things to keep in mind:

Ability to Harmonize

A good background vocalist has a good ear for harmony and is able to hold their part while the person next to them is singing something else. If a prospective background singer is not able to hold their own part when singing with others, they should not sing in your band, no matter how great a voice they have.

Ability to Blend

The fact that every human voice is unique is a great and glorious miracle. However, when selecting background singers, choose folks who are able to blend well and will create a uniform sound when singing together. It often helps to choose singers with similar vocal timbres. This is why many great performers (Prince and Stevie Wonder, for example) often sing their own background vocals in the studio.

Compatibility of Articulation

What you are looking for in a background vocal sound is something that speaks as one voice. No individual voice should stick out, or the effect will be spoiled. This means that all the words sung by the background vocalists should be pronounced in precisely the same manner, with the same accents and timing.

ARRANGING FOR BACKGROUND VOCALS

Create background vocals that form easy-to-hear intervals. Thirds, sixths, and triads are best. When three voices sing a major triad together (Do Mi Sol), a pleasing resonance is created that makes three voices sound like a whole choir. In figure 8.1, the black notes represent the lead vocals. Open notes indicate background vocals. These different chord voicings will all sound pleasing.

Fig. 8.1. Triad Voicing

Getting the backing vocals in synch is potentially one of the most challenging aspects of rehearsing a band. Help yourself out by creating background lines that sit naturally in the voice and are easy to sing.

Remember our discussion of notation basics in chapter 2? The smallest distance between two notes is a half step. The next smallest distance is a whole step. When creating background vocals, it is best to write each line as if it was a melody in its own right. That way, they will all be easier to sing and to remember. Though there are always exceptions to the rule, a good melody moves more often by steps than by skips.

Listen carefully to the following two background lines against the same lead melody. In the first example, the background lines move in awkward leaps, and the voices are constantly crossing each other. In the second example, the background lines move in a smooth and stepwise manner. Which one sounds better to you?

TRACK 18

(a) Moving by Skip

TRACK 19

(b) Moving by Step

Fig. 8.3. Background Vocal Parts

Digital Arranging

In today's high tech environment, it is possible to create a perfectly decent song using only a computer and a good MIDI keyboard. Computer programs such as Finale, Pro Tools, Reason, and Logic allow the arranger to layer track upon track, creating an entire electronic symphony. Indeed, electronic keyboards today contain such accurate imitations of instrumental sounds that even a sophisticated listener is often fooled.

Does this mean that the information you have acquired so far about the functions of the instruments in the band must be thrown out the window? Not at all. Although the instruments and methods of sound production have changed, the principles of arranging remain very much the same. The bass and drums still provide the groove, the keyboard and guitar still lay down the harmony, and soloists will still provide pacing and dramatic emphasis. As you arrange your material, you can make use of these basic principles while taking advantage of the tremendous range of electronic sounds available today.

COMMERCIALLY AVAILABLE BACKING TRACKS

There are many CDs and Web sites that offer backing tracks to songs, whether they are pop, rock, jazz, show tunes, or gospel. Now that you know what each member of the band is supposed to do, you will be in a much better position to select the highest quality tracks. Before purchasing any tracks, listen to them carefully with the function of each instrument in mind.

Do the bass and drums adequately recreate the groove? Is the comping by either synthesizer, guitar, or piano sufficient for you to hear the harmony clearly?

You will also want to make sure that the track is in the proper key and tempo for you. Never just go along with the flow, singing something in the wrong key or tempo just because that's the way it is on the track.

You now know how to make a new lead sheet in your preferred key. Once you've got your lead sheet, you can take it to any qualified accompanist or musical group and create your own custom backing track.

Remember, knowledge is power. The more you know about how to get your song *exactly* the way you need to have it, the stronger your performance will be.

CHAPTER 9

Rehearsing Your Band

SUZIE AND THE BAND: A HORROR STORY

After months of pestering her Uncle Harry, Suzie Q finally got her band a gig at the Elks Club dinner dance. For weeks before the show, Suzie and her friends had been putting up posters around town. Five hundred tickets had already been sold.

For the past three months, Suzie and her voice teacher had been hard at work preparing her repertoire of dance favorites. Painstakingly, she had created lead sheets for each song transposed into the best keys for her voice. Now it was time for her first rehearsal with the band.

Since she lived in a small studio apartment, Suzie was grateful when the drummer suggested they practice at his place. Since all the guys in the band had late gigs the night before, it was agreed that practice would begin at 3:00 P.M.

Arriving at the drummer's house on the appointed day, Suzie was greeted and invited into the kitchen for a few beers. The two of them spent the next half hour chilling and listening to the latest Jill Scott CD.

After a while, the bass player and lead guitarist wandered in and proceeded to regale the group with a hilarious story about the tightfisted owner of the nightclub down the street. By this time, it was 4:30 and the keyboard player had still not shown up. After repeated calls to his cell phone went unanswered, Suzie decided to begin rehearsal without him.

The guitar and bass players plugged into their amps and cranked the volume dials to 10. With an authoritative crash on his cymbals, the drummer laid into a hard rock groove and the band began to jam furiously. Excited by the group's high energy, Suzie joined in, singing with gusto. Although the drummer had no sound system, the lead guitar player let Suzie plug her mic into one channel of his guitar amp. She couldn't really hear herself, but what the heck! The music was on fire, and she was a part of it.

After jamming on a one-chord vamp for an hour, Suzie felt the group was sufficiently warmed up to begin rehearsing her song. By this time, it was after 6:00 P.M. Halfway into the first verse, the bass player's cell phone chimed. It was his girlfriend asking him to pick up some groceries on the way home. The rest of the band waited patiently while he and his girlfriend had a fifteen-minute argument about whose job it was to run the errands in the family. Just as the bass player finished his call, the drummer's five-year-old twins burst into the room to demonstrate their two-person version of "Wipe-Out" on the tom toms.

Twenty minutes later, after the kids were shooed out by the drummer's wife, band practice resumed. It was now 7:00 P.M., and they hadn't really rehearsed any of the twenty songs on Suzie's set list. At 7:30, the guitar and bass players packed up their equipment and left for their gig at a club across town.

By this time, Suzie could hear the drummer's kids screaming upstairs and knew it was time to call it a night. They hadn't accomplished as much as they'd hoped, but there was still a week left before the show. . . .

GETTING THE MOST OUT OF BAND PRACTICE

I hope that Suzie got through her Big Gig okay. Based on the above scenario, however, I tend to doubt it. I don't deny it's great fun to hang out with friends and jam. But in the world of professional music, time is money. Having and sticking to a clear, well-organized rehearsal plan is the best way to insure a solid performance on gig night.

Here's a list of tips that would have helped Suzie get more out of her rehearsal time.

1. Use an appropriate rehearsal venue.

    Find a place to rehearse where you won't disturb others and others won't disturb you. If you have to practice in the living room, make sure that the rest of the family understands that this time is sacred time, not to be interrupted by phone calls, children, etc., except in the case of direst emergency.

    You are asking your bandmates to commit some of their valuable time to practice with you. Frequent interruptions waste time and dissipate the energy of the group. Take yourself and your music seriously enough to devote quality time to the rehearsal process.

2. Rehearse in conditions as close as possible to that of the performance.

    If you are planning to perform in a local auditorium and it is possible to rent the space for a couple of run-throughs before the day of the show, by all means do so. Getting comfortable with the performance space ahead of time will increase the odds of you giving your best performance.

    If access to the performance venue is not possible prior to the show, at the very least, be sure that you use a good sound system when practicing with the band. Your comfort level at the show will increase tremendously if you already have a realistic idea of what you are going to sound like when the band is pumping at full volume.

Don't try to sing over the band, even in practice, without using a sound system. Doing so is a sure recipe for wearing out your voice. Remember that your band needs to hear you clearly in order to create the best accompaniment possible.

3. Have an agenda for each rehearsal.

The best musicians are busy people like yourself who don't have a lot of time to waste. Set a realistic goal for what you hope to accomplish within the time available and then stick to your schedule. If other things come up during the course of practice, make note of them and put them on the schedule for the next rehearsal.

Here is one possible plan that Suzie could have used to better organize her rehearsal time.

SUZIE'S REHEARSAL AGENDA

Goal: Rehearse three tunes for next week's gig at the Elks Club.

3:00 P.M. sharp–3:15	Band members arrive at drummer's place and set up.
3:15–3:30	Play through tune 1 and identify problem areas.
3:30-4:00	Rehearse and fix problem areas in tune 1.

Note: Any individual problems not fixed at this time should be practiced at home by the band member in question so that it is ready to go at the next rehearsal.

4:00–4:15	Play through tune 2 and identify problem areas.
4:15–4:45	Rehearse and fix problem areas in tune 2.
4:45–5:00	Break. Step outside, get a smoke, use the toilet, whatever.
5:00 sharp–5:15	Play through tune 3 and identify problem areas.
5:15–5:45	Rehearse and fix problems in tune 3.
5:45–6:00	Discuss what each band member will do to get ready for the next rehearsal.
6:00 sharp	Rehearsal concludes.

Practice sessions don't always go as smoothly as planned. People are only human, after all, and things happen. But if Suzie had gone into her rehearsal with some semblance of a plan, she would have been a lot better prepared for her show.

TECHNIQUES FOR EFFECTIVE REHEARSAL

Now that you have gotten yourself and your band organized, you can use some of the practice techniques you learned in chapter 5 to make your rehearsals more effective.

Isolate the Problem Area

Pay close attention as you sing through your piece. If you notice that something doesn't sound right, stop immediately and locate the problem area. Is the problem in the chorus? The verse? Which measure?

Find the Source of the Problem

If you are certain that the problem is not with your own vocals, listen to the band play through the section in question without singing. Once you know what each instrument in the rhythm section should be doing, specific mistakes will be easier to identify.

Is the problem with the melody? In that case, you'll want to rehearse the background singers alone. Is there a problem with the groove? Ask the bass and drums to play alone. If the issue seems to be with the song's harmony, isolating the keys and guitar will help.

Tactfully Correct the Problem

Once you've identified the mistake, be precise about what you want your musicians to change. Bandmates will be less resistant to suggestions if they are specific and come from a place of solid musical knowledge. Be as tactful as you can. Obviously, mistakes must be pointed out and corrected. But you'll get more out of your band if you avoid embarrassing them or putting them on the spot when making criticisms.

Tempos, Cues, Starting, and Stopping

The two most important parts of your performance are its first and last notes. The way your first song begins sets the tone for your entire performance. The ending of your last song will be the last thing the audience takes away from your show. To give an effective performance, you must know how to start and end your songs.

Starting Your Song

To determine your song's speed, or "tempo," sing through the chorus in your mind while tapping your foot to the beat. If its time signature is 4/4 (see chapter 2), then you would count "one... two... one two three four" in the rhythm of two half notes and four quarter notes to indicate this tempo to the band.

To get your song off to a strong start, be sure to give your band a clear and rhythmically solid count-off. In time signatures other than 4/4, a two-measure count-off will get the band started effectively. For example, in 3/4 you could count "one two three" in rhythm for two measures.

Polished Endings

To avoid overly abrupt endings, many songs slow down somewhat before the final note is played. This is particularly true in live performance, where "fade-out" endings are generally impractical.

To have the band slow down and end together as a unit, someone will need to cue the ending by using a raised arm to indicate the timing of the last few notes. In a large ensemble, the music director, keyboardist, or bandleader performs this function. In a smaller ensemble, however, you will be required to cue the band and control how your song comes to an end.

Even if you have the luxury of a music director to conduct your band, you should still be aware of how this is done. The more you know about all aspects of your performance, the greater control you will have over its ultimate outcome. Just remember the singer's mantra: knowledge is power.

When cueing the band, your gestures must:

a. Be easily visible. Make sure that your arm movements are large enough to be seen by everyone in your group.

b. Be clear and definite. Avoid uncontrolled arm movements. A good back-up band watches your every move, so when you are ready to indicate the end of your song, there must be no doubt about your intentions.

c. Come from an awareness of what the band is already playing. Failure to follow this principle creates a jarring effect similar to that of cutting off someone in mid-sentence. If the band is vamping a four-measure phrase (remember our discussion of vamps in chapter 4), finish the phrase before ending the song.

PART II

Presentation

CHAPTER 10

Auditions

Singing for an audition differs from other kinds of performing in that it's far more of a precision activity. In a five-minute audition, mistakes that would be overlooked in the context of a longer performance become glaringly obvious.

In an audition, many key aspects of your performance are out of your control. The music you sing may have been chosen by someone else. You may have to work with an accompanist you've never seen before, or sing a song a capella when it should have accompaniment. You may be abruptly stopped in the middle or asked to sing something differently than you prepared it. Whether you are Cool Hand Luke under pressure or a Nervous Nellie like me, the principles in this chapter will help you hone your audition skills.

THE TEN BASIC PRINCIPLES OF AUDITIONING

1. It's not about you. It's about them.

    When taking an audition, remind yourself that the judges are only evaluating your suitability for a specific musical situation. The audition is *not* about you as a person, or even about your talent or ability to function in a musical situation other than the one for which you are auditioning.

    The audition process is about *them* (the judges) and *their* agenda. They are looking for a particular musical skill set, and their evaluation of you is based solely on these criteria.

2. An opinion is only an opinion, not gospel.

    There are many stories of famous singers who were rejected by audition committees at some point along the way. Legend has it that Barbra Streisand was thrown out of her high school choir. Diva Jennifer Hudson was bounced from *American Idol* just a few months before landing her starring role in *Dreamgirls*. As an educator, I have learned to never—*never*—tell a student that he or she is not suited for a career in music. There are just too many variables out there. Life is unpredictable, music industry trends change, and people grow and mature in surprising ways.

So never take as gospel the opinions of judges at auditions. They are talking from their own very limited vantage point and are truly not in the best position to evaluate your future growth or potential. Always give yourself the gift of believing in your dreams. You may not be cut out for the particular situation for which you have auditioned, but if you really want to sing, there will always be a place for you somewhere.

3. Knowledge is power.

    When you get feedback from audition judges, teachers, or any other knowledgeable source, take time to study what has been said. If you can accept the pronouncements of the judges as just opinions, nothing more, you will be less defensive and better able to learn from their comments.

    If you truly want to win your next audition before these judges, you will need to understand their criteria. What are they looking for? If you came up short in an area that is important to them, it's good to find that out so you have a chance to rectify the problem before your next audition.

    Criticism never stops, whether it comes from teachers, peers, friends, or music reviewers. The important thing is to develop a balanced mind set that maintains self-esteem while remaining open to criticism. It is a tricky proposition, but one well worth undertaking if you plan to enjoy your life as a performer.

4. Know and follow the rules and expectations for your particular audition to the letter.

    This is a logical extension of the "Knowledge Is Power" principle. Most auditions have specific requirements about how many songs you can sing and how long they should be. If they want you to sing two contrasting songs, don't bring three ballads. If they want you to sing for no more than three minutes, don't bring a ten-minute aria.

    Some people will come into the audition feeling that their beauty and talent will cause the committee to make an exception to the rules in their case. In my twenty years of auditioning singers, I have rarely seen this happen.

    The rules are the rules, and they are there for a reason. In an average day auditioning prospective students for Berklee, my committee listens to a new candidate every fifteen minutes—perhaps twenty or thirty per day. During that time, we hear each one perform, sight-read, improvise, and demonstrate their ear training skills, and then we make a determination as to their eligibility for our program. With such a schedule, there is very little "wiggle room" or tolerance for people who want to be the "exception to the rule."

    Bottom line: Know as much as you can about what will be expected of you before you walk into the audition, and then abide by the guidelines that you are given.

5. Prepare thoroughly with these expectations in mind.

    Once you know what the judges are asking for, your job is to prepare as thoroughly as you can. Preparation is the key to success in any endeavor. If you have not prepared your music to the best of your ability, you cannot be upset if the results reflect your lack of commitment.

6. Stay in the moment.

Most of us have a shrill little voice inside that gives us a constant running commentary as we perform. You know the voice, I am sure: "Well you got through the scale passage okay, but look out! Here comes the high note. . . . The judges must hate me; look at the way they are staring, blah, blah, etc. etc." The more we start listening to that voice, the more distracted and self-conscious we will become.

The most important moment in any audition is the moment you're in. If you have made a hideous blunder the measure before, let it go. If you sang the previous measure better than you have ever sung it before, let it go. Think of yourself as William Tell, shooting an apple off your son's head with your bow and arrow. If your concentration leaves the present moment, someone is very likely to wind up dead.

7. Pay attention, and remain flexible.

When we are under pressure, we often become so focused on ourselves that we fail to pay attention to important cues from our listeners. When judging a contestant's performance in an audition, I sometimes make suggestions to them that would help them improve their performance.

A common example is the person who starts off their song at a tempo that is much faster than they are capable of sustaining. I will say to that person: "Slow down. Think about your correct tempo, and try your song again." If they are unable to be in the moment and pay attention, they will frequently restart the song at the same breakneck speed.

Sometimes during the audition, I'll ask someone to improvise over the chords to their song, or to try singing it in a different key or style. If they are not able to pay attention and adapt, they will score poorly on this part of the audition. Never allow yourself to get so rigid musically that you can't try something new on the spur of the moment. And the first step is to be aware of what is going on around you.

8. Leave as little to chance as possible.

Get to the hall early—make that *way* early.

There is *nothing* more stressful than being late for an important performance. MapQuest the venue, and plan your transportation well before the event. If necessary, drive there the day before to scout things out. Is there parking? Build in extra time in case the traffic is terrible, the subway is slow, or your ride is late.

Have all the materials you will need with you.

Pack a "gig bag" the day before with everything you will need: your mic, extra copies of the music, backing CD, etc. If your tracks are on CD and you are not sure there will be a CD player there, bring a boom box with you. If you have your tracks on an iPod or some other MP3 device, bring whatever cables and adapters are needed to plug it into the sound system. Leave as little to chance as possible.

9. Look and feel your best.

Dress in clothes that suit the part for which you are aspiring *and* that make you feel confident. If you are the type that likes to come in full make-up or a suit and tie, do so. If you are a blue jeans type like me, try to find an outfit that looks sharp enough to impress but feels comfortable enough to put you at ease.

Get enough rest. Avoid stressful people and situations as much as possible the day before the audition. I know that this can be easier said than done, but if this performance is a priority for you, now's the time to walk your talk. You can't sing your best if you are distracted or upset. Focus and commitment are two of the most important qualities you can cultivate in your quest for excellence.

10. Project positive energy and confidence.

Everyone is nervous when taking an audition. There would probably be something seriously wrong with you if you were not. The question is not how to avoid getting nervous feelings, but how to handle them when they arise.

Remember that once you step into the audition room, all the work is over. Now it's time to simply do what you have done before countless times in the practice room. The more fun you have performing, the more fun the judgeswill have listening to you and the better the vibe will be all around.

If you have taken to heart the tips that I have outlined in the preceding chapters, you will be as ready as you can be for what will be asked of you. What more can you do? This is your fifteen minutes of fame. The time has come to savor every minute of it.

DRESSING FOR AUDITIONS

When dressing for an audition, take into account the role for which you are auditioning. Whether it is for a TV appearance, a band, or a Broadway show, what you wear should help the judges imagine you in the desired role. If you are going for a show, dress like the character you hope to portray. If you are trying out for a band, do some research to find out their particular look and style and dress appropriately.

If it is a contest or school audition, specific attire is somewhat less important. Of course, you will want to look neat and clean. I also recommend that you wear an outfit in which you can sing comfortably. Avoid tight belts or any other items that might restrict your breathing.

Beyond that, you should wear whatever will give you the greatest feeling of self-assurance before the judges. If you have a pair of lucky socks or a favorite earring that makes you feel like a star, then go for it!

If you have any doubt about what to wear for an important competition, contact its sponsoring organization and enquire. There's nothing worse than arriving to perform and realizing that you are inappropriately dressed for the occasion. But, if you should arrive in jeans and everyone else is in a tux, don't let your discomfort get in the way of giving the finest musical performance you can on stage. When it's all said and done, the judges are more interested in how your music sounds than anything else.

TIPS FROM BERKLEE'S AUDITION EXPERTS

At Berklee, I am fortunate to work with many faculty members who have shared my experience of auditioning hundreds—even thousands—of students. Here are some of their thoughts on audition preparation:

Professor Jetro da Silva is known here as the "accompanist to the stars." He has worked with Patti LaBelle, Celine Dion, Earth Wind and Fire, Whitney Houston, Stevie Wonder, and many others. Here are some of his thoughts on how to prepare for an audition:

"The most important thing is to have a strong sense of self-esteem and to project a positive, 'can-do' attitude. When people select a background singer, they are looking for someone they can get along with for long stretches on the road. If they sense that you are going to be a problem, no matter how well you sing, you will not get the gig.

You can't control what people feel about you. You will not always have the perfect/right 'chemistry' in the particular person's opinion. Never let anyone's opinion of you dictate who you are."

Jetro also advises preparing in detail for the specific gig situation you desire.

*"You should know all the group's songs, including **all** the background vocal parts, not just the ones that you normally would sing for your voice type. And it is crucial that you know how to blend well with other singers."*

Three Different Kinds of Auditions

Jetro likes to list three basic kinds of auditions:

1. The "Business Event." In this kind of audition, the committee already knows who the winner will be, but for whatever reason, they want to hold an audition anyway. Even though you will probably not win, this kind of audition is important to take. They are a way to network and to be heard, so always be prepared to give your best. You never know who may be listening.
2. The "All About the Look" audition. In this kind of audition, the judges may not have a clue what they are looking for musically, but they have a visual concept for the band. The winner of this kind of audition will be the one who looks right for the gig. If you have done your research thoroughly, you will arrive at your audition wearing the clothes, hairstyle, and accessories that reflect the style of the band you hope to join.

3. The Musical Audition. In this kind of audition, music is the top priority. You must flat out be the best singer in the room to get the gig.

Since you do not always know in advance which kind of audition you will be walking into, thorough preparation in all three areas is the best policy. "And remember," Jetro advises, "the decision may be made by the person above the one who is auditioning you, so don't take things too personally. Never let their expectations and judgments define who you are."

More Tips

Here are some tips from a few of my other colleagues here.

"People who are confident, comfortable, and able to engage an audience do far better at their auditions, even if they do not have the best voice. If there is going to be a band at your audition, be sure to practice your song either alone or (better still) with live accompaniment before your audition. Too many people rely on hearing the accompaniment exactly as it is on their backing track and are thrown off if they have to perform with live musicians."
—Associate Professor Nancy Morris, Singer/Songwriter; performances on Nashville's TNN network, and with artists including Lee Greenwood, Brenda Lee, and Radney Foster)

"The one aspect of auditioning that is always under your control is the song you choose. Often people choose a song they think will sound great as a part of the Singer's Showcase concerts. It's better to choose a song specifically for the audition, and then if you are selected to participate, you can pick a different song for the performance. Your audition song should put your best foot forward, so choose something that shows your voice to its best advantage. Also bear in mind that your audition time is limited. Be ready to sing the strongest two minutes of your song, rather than starting from the beginning."
—Professor Ken Zambello, Music Director for Berklee's acclaimed Singer's Showcase; performances with artists including the Coasters, the Belmonts, the Four Aces, and Frankie Ford

"Too many singers are unable to perform when they get nervous, but if you are well prepared, you will be able to overcome your nerves and sing. Also, it's important to develop your own personal style. Remain true to your own identity, and choose songs that are in accordance with that identity."
—Rob Rose, Associate Vice President for Special Programs

"Having a good sound is just the beginning. Be musically literate. Learn to play the piano if possible, and develop your skills as an all-around musician."
—Greg Badolato, Assistant Vice President of International Programs, and Head of Berklee's Audition and Interview Activities

CHAPTER 11

Getting a Good Sound: Microphones, PAs, and Sound Checks

As a vocalist, your sound system is your best friend. A great microphone can make a mediocre voice sound wonderful. On the other hand, even the most fabulous vocalist can sound ragged or shrill with poor sound reinforcement.

SELECTING YOUR FIRST MICROPHONE

There are a several kinds of mics available. If you are just getting started, my suggestion is to purchase a sturdy, all-around microphone that will withstand the stress of repeated use. When shopping for one, here are some things to investigate before you buy.

1. Does this mic effectively amplify my full range?

    When trying out a mic, try singing through the entire range of your voice: low to high and then back down. Does it sound full and rich throughout? Some microphones will sound scratchy or trebly on the high notes. Others will emphasize the middle overtones of your voice but not produce all high and low overtones accurately. There are a lot of semi-toy, karaoke-type mics out there that are just not professional quality. Be sure to test any mic thoroughly before purchasing. If there is more than one microphone in your price range, try them all before making your decision. You are looking for a mic that will produce a clear sound throughout your singing range.

2. Will this mic work well with the most common kinds of PA systems?

Look for a mic that is a low impedance microphone. It will have a three-prong end. You will need a XLR (three prong) mic cord. A heavy gauge cord will conduct the sound better than a thinner cord. Avoid mics that come with the cords attached or that only plug into a quarter-inch plug, as they will not be able to give you a full sound.

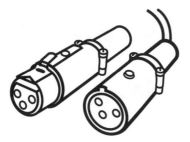

Fig. 11.1. XLR Connectors for Vocal Mic Cord

3. Does this mic need an additional power source ("phantom power") to be effective?

There are several kinds of microphones that are used for live performance. The two most common types are the dynamic and the condenser mic.

For your first microphone, I recommend a dynamic microphone. Dynamic microphones are popular with many singers because they are very durable while being quite reasonable in price. A Shure SM58 dynamic microphone is a good choice when you are first beginning your singing career.

Fig. 11.2. Shure SM58 Dynamic Microphone. One of the most popular mics. (Photo used with permission from Shure Corp.)

Condenser microphones require additional power or "phantom power." Many recognized pop/rock artists use condenser microphones in high profile performances because of their sensitivity of picking up sound and low distortion even at high volumes. Be aware, however, that condenser mics tend to be more sensitive to changes in temperature and humidity than dynamic mics and require more delicate handling.

Cordless Mics

Cordless condenser mics have become increasingly common. Their advantages are obvious. No longer constrained by a cord, you can move, groove, and reach out directly to your audience. Instead of using a cable, a wireless mic sends the sound from your microphone to a receiver on a specific frequency. The *receiver* then transmits this frequency into your PA.

Because they transmit UHF and VHF signals, using a cordless mic can sometimes be complicated. Your signal may not be picked up clearly by the receiver, or you may begin picking up other signals. Either one of these situations may cause sound interference. When purchasing a cordless system, look for one where the whole setup (including receiver) is dependable, with minimum sound transmission interference.

This technology is evolving quickly, so research the current different types and models available to select the one that best meets your needs.

Headsets

If you are going to move around a lot or need your hands free to play another instrument while singing, a headset system might suit you. Headsets can be wireless—complete with a receiver and battery pack—or they can be wired, like handheld microphones. It's important to check the different models and types of headset microphones to ensure that the headset fits you well and is able to pick up your vocal sound clearly.

Another alternative is wireless lavalier (or lapel) mics. These are often used by singers/actors in a stage setting and sometimes used by performers who dance while singing. Like all cordless systems, these mics must be used with a transmitter/receiver and come in a wide array of price ranges.

USING YOUR MICROPHONE

The first thing to know about any microphone is how to position yourself to get the best sound. Most handheld mics used for vocal performance are *unidirectional*. These mics will only amplify sounds that come into them from one direction. Some microphones are *omnidirectional*; they pick up sound from any direction.

In practical terms, this means that you must take care to sing directly into the axis or "sweet spot" of the mic in order to be fully amplified. For most stage mics, the sweet spot is accessed by singing directly into the top of the ball that covers it. For some studio mics, this spot is on the side of the microphone.

(a) Top-Address Mic   (b) Side-Address Mic

Fig. 11.3. Positions for (a) Top- and (b) Side-Address Mics

To get comfortable with a new microphone, you will need to experiment with your vocal delivery. Generally speaking, when you begin to sing louder, you will move the mic a little farther away while still being heard in the PA system speakers. For soft, intimate passages, get close to the microphone. Moving the mic even an inch will make a big difference in how much of your voice is picked up.

There is no one set distance that is applicable for all situations. Within the same song, a good singer may make hundreds of subtle adjustments in mic placement to get the desired result. Only through practice and experience will you be able to find the right placement.

PA SYSTEMS

A PA (public address) system is the unit that carries your voice out to the audience. It does this by powering (usually two) speakers. Before purchasing a PA system, give serious thought to the size of the room that you typically play, your band size (duo vs. ten musicians), and your vocal style and delivery.

AMPS AND MIXERS

Live performers usually use one of two PA mixer/amp setups to power speakers. A *self-powered mixer* comes in one piece; it is both a mixer and an amplifier. The self-powered mixer is easily portable with minimum setup. You can bring a self-powered unit, plug in your speakers, and you are ready to perform!

For larger performing venues where sound coverage and quality are crucial, separate mixer and amplifier components are used. In either setup (self-powered or separate components), many mixers include a small digital reverb that is built into the unit. Reverb (short for reverberation) creates the auditory illusion that you are singing in a large room or concert hall, and gives your vocal sound additional body and warmth. If your mixer does not contain reverb, most systems allow you to add a separate digital reverb unit. Below is an example of what the mixing board looks like.

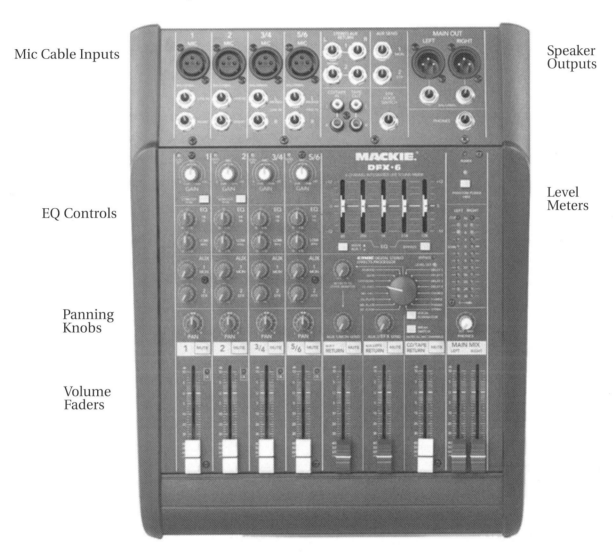

Mic Cable Inputs

Speaker Outputs

EQ Controls

Level Meters

Panning Knobs

Volume Faders

Fig. 11.4. Mixer

SPEAKERS AND MONITORS

The last component of your PA system is your speakers. Quality speakers are essential for an accurate production of your vocal sound. The louder the performance and the bigger the room, the more speakers you will need to carry the sound to the audience. When purchasing speakers, make sure that they are compatible with your system's amplifier. If you are buying your sound system as a unit, this should not be a problem, but when buying separate components, check the watts per channel capacity of both the amp and the speaker to make sure they can be used together. It's no use buying big speakers if your amplifier is not powerful enough to drive them. Similarly, a too-powerful amp can blow out speakers that are too small.

Another key factor to consider is the portability of your system. If you are doing a lot of gigging, you will be loading and unloading, setting up and breaking down this system many, many times. Try out several types of speakers before purchasing.

Monitors

Monitor speakers allow you to hear your sound when you are onstage. If you are singing and playing by yourself or with one other musician, you may not need monitors. But if you have a high-energy band, monitors will help you to hear yourself more clearly. They also will help prevent you from over-singing! Here is diagram of how a speaker and monitor setup might look for a band with a rhythm section, lead vocalist, and three backup singers. Note that the main PA speakers should always be set up in front of the microphones to avoid feedback.

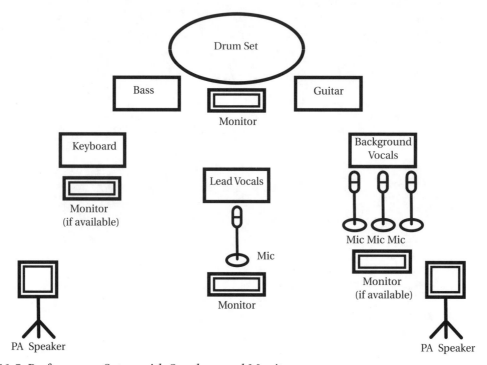

Fig 11.5. Performance Setup with Speakers and Monitors

SOUND CHECKS

The day of the show has arrived. You've set up your PA and mics. Here are some things to keep in mind as you do your sound check.

Appoint a Designated Listener

When you are checking your sound, what may sound great to you onstage through the monitors might sound terrible in the house and vice versa. If at all possible, have a reliable person listen specifically for your voice from a number of different places in the auditorium. Ideally, there will be a sound engineer on your gig whose job it is to make you and your band sound good. However, on many gigs, you will have to rely on a friend or someone else in the band for this purpose. If there is no one else who can provide you with an extra set of ears, you can walk out away from the band and listen to how you sound in the speakers, as long as you have either a wireless mic or one with a cord over 25 feet long.

Either you or your designated listener should be listening for three specific things, related to how the vocals sound:

1. Are the lead vocals prominent in the mix?

    Your band, horn section, and background vocalists are all important parts of your sound. But as the lead vocalist, you are the star. You should always be clearly heard over anything else that may be going on.

2. What is the quality of your voice?

    If your voice is coming through a PA system, a great deal can be done to alter your sound by using EQ and reverb. So have your "designated listener" really pay close attention to the way your voice sounds. Is it shrill and metallic? Maybe you need to turn down the treble. Is it muddy, lacking definition? In this case, reducing the low- and mid-range sounds may help. Reverb can give your voice an added warmth and richness, but be careful. Too much reverb will make you sound like you are singing in a cave. Also, be aware that your amplified voice will sound differently when the hall is empty than when it is full. Effects added to your voice in an empty auditorium may sound exaggerated, but when the same auditorium is filled, they may sound just right.

3. How is the group's overall volume level? Is there any unintentional distortion or feedback?

    When doing a sound check, I want the sound crew to be prepared to handle the full dynamic range of my material. I will have my group play something soft and intimate, and then something loud and intense. I am checking to make sure that nothing will distort or feed back in the heat of performance. Nothing says "amateur" more than an unexpected feedback episode during a gig. If you have no sound person and must troubleshoot for feedback on your own, double-check to make sure that no mics are facing directly into your speakers (see figure 11.5). In the heat of performance, this obvious source of feedback is often overlooked.

Know When Enough Is Enough

Once you have established some general levels for the band as a whole, run through the beginnings and endings of two or three of your most challenging songs. Once everyone can hear themselves clearly and you know your voice sounds okay, your sound check has accomplished its purpose.

The tendency to get into a more serious rehearsal during a sound check is strong. For one thing, you are finally onstage and can hear everything that's going on clearly. For another, your adrenaline is pumping as you realize that the performance you have worked so long for is almost here.

I cannot tell you strongly enough—after you have gotten everyone comfortable with their sound onstage, STOP. In just a few hours, you will be performing your show before a live and appreciative audience. Material rehearsed desperately at the last minute during a sound check is rarely remembered during the heat of performance. Stop and give yourself a chance to rest and gather energy for the show.

CHAPTER 12

Warm Up

When we are performing, it is easy to get so focused on externals that we miss the hints our body may be giving us of impending vocal exhaustion. When you sing, check in with your body by asking yourself the following questions:

1. How's my posture?

    We all know that we should stand so that our breath and energy flows freely through the body. In the heat of performance, it is easy to forget.

    Take a look at the following picture. Does this resemble you?

Fig. 12.1. Poor Singing Posture

Here's how you want to look:

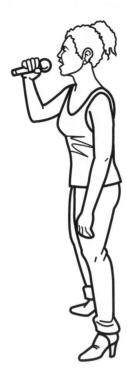

Fig. 12.2. Good Singing Posture

Practice in front of a mirror will help you to develop greater body awareness and eliminate bad habits.

2. How's my breathing? Am I breathing?

    To sing your best, your breath should feel like it's coming from your abdomen. But when we are nervous, we sometimes forget to breathe deeply, taking only shallow "chest-deep" breaths instead. Even if you need to breathe more often in the phrase than you normally would, be sure that your breath is coming from a deep and supported place. If you have been practicing vocal exercises faithfully, this kind of breathing will become second nature, even when you are under stress.

3. How's my physical tension level?

    Do you find your fists clenching or your jaw or neck tightening? Do you grimace and hunch your shoulders? All these things are signs of physical tension that can drain vital energy from your voice during performance. Once again, practicing in front of a mirror will help you to become aware of these habits.

4. How does my voice feel?

    Does your voice feel tired? Is your throat raw and scratchy? Does it hurt? Do certain notes tighten up and not want to speak freely? Don't ignore these signals from your body. It may be time to back off, rest your voice, and consult with your teacher about how best to proceed.

CAROLYN'S TEN-MINUTE WARM-UP

Before you launch into your show, it's important to get your body and mind in the right condition.

Here is the ten-minute warm-up that I use before doing any serious singing.

Stretch, Bend, and Shake

1. Inhale, raise your arms over your head, stand on tiptoe, and stretch as tall as possible.
2. Exhale and bend over at the waist. Let your fingers dangle to the floor.
3. Stay in this position and inhale.
4. Exhale and shake out your arms and shoulders.
5. Inhale and stand up.

Repeat three times.

Fig. 12.3. Stretch, Bend, and Shake

Neck Roll

1. Stand with head and spine straight and weight evenly balanced.
2. Gently roll your neck three times to the right, then three times to the left.
   Take care not to arch your neck too far when rolling towards the back.

Now repeat this exercise while yawning deeply.

Fig. 12.4. Neck Roll

Shoulder Shrug

1. Inhale as you shrug your shoulders up to your ears.
2. Exhale and sigh as you allow them to drop. Do this a few times until you feel your shoulders relax.

Fig. 12.5. Shoulder Shrug

Slap Front and Back

1. Keeping your arms totally relaxed, stand with your feet shoulder-length apart.
2. Gently turn your waist from side to side, allowing your arms to slap across your front and back as you turn.
3. As you do this, buzz your lips and make a sound like a motorboat (lip trill).

Fig. 12.6. Slap Front and Back

Propping the Heavens

1. Stand with feet shoulder-width apart.
2. With palms facing the ceiling, raise your hands along the centerline of your body.
3. When your hands get to the level of your throat, press the tips of your middle fingers together and rotate the hands as you continue to raise them up over your head, fingers touching, palms facing the ceiling.
4. Exhale and separate your hands. As you slowly lower your arms to your side, palms facing toward the floor, sing "ahh" on any pitch. Repeat three times.

Fig. 12.7. Propping the Heavens

Swing Arms and Drop

1. Feet shoulder-width apart, inhale and rise up on your toes as you raise your arms to shoulder level.
2. Exhale forcefully as you swing your arms and drop down on your heels.
3. Repeat this exercise three more times and say "ha" vigorously with full voice as you swing your arms down and drop down on your heels.

Fig. 12.8. Swing Arms and Drop

Trembling Horse

1. Stand with feet shoulder-width. Starting from the ground up, begin quivering. Imagine energy rising up through your legs, waist, torso, and arms.
2. As the energy moves through, allow it to vibrate your body. Shake as the spirit moves you. Do this three times, then shake out any tension from your arms and legs.
3. Stand quietly and let your energy settle as you breathe deep into your belly.

From this place, your body and mind are now ready to begin vocalizing more seriously. If you have time, go on to practice your favorite vocal warm-ups. In a pinch, you are ready to go do the gig.

Fig. 12.9. Trembling Horse

CHAPTER 13

Overcoming Performance Anxiety

When I was twelve, my choir director asked me to sing a solo for the seventh grade assembly. Although I felt reasonably confident in the wings before going on, my knees locked and my breath disappeared the minute I stepped out on the stage. As I opened my mouth to sing, a weird palsy-like shaking overtook my body. I was only able to sing two wobbly lines before fleeing in tears. Needless to say, my performance was the talk of the school for months afterward, and it was a long time before I was able to sing in public again.

Nowadays, though I still get very keyed up before important shows, I have managed to eliminate the most crippling effects of stage fright from my performances. In this chapter, I'll teach you a simple three-step approach to overcoming performance anxiety.

Step 1. Calm Your Body

Though we no longer have to survive in the jungle as our primitive ancestors once did, our bodies still respond to *any* stressful situation—in this case, singing in front of an audience—as a matter of life and death. Once this "fight or flight" response is triggered, our physical system is automatically flooded with an energy-boosting chemical called adrenaline.

When an adrenaline rush hits you, it's difficult to remain physically calm. Though well-meaning souls will tell you to "calm down" or "relax," I recommend that you go with the flow. You feel like you could run around the block twice? Fine. This is a perfectly natural response.

Instead of getting all sweaty running around the block, try the exercises that follow. They are designed to help dispel excess nervous energy.

Arm Swing

Stand with your feet shoulder-width apart. With your hands relaxed and loose, inhale deeply, as you raise your arms with palms facing down to shoulder height. As you do this, imagine that you are breathing into your abdomen all the energy of the universe. Now, exhale forcefully as you swing your arms down and back. When you exhale, imagine that you are releasing any excess energy, nerves, and bad vibes. Do this several times in rhythm until you feel more centered.

Shake It Out

Shake as if you were a wet dog throwing water off your body. Shake your legs out one by one. Shake your arms. Then allow yourself to move in free form however it feels best.

Step 2. Calm Your Emotions

After you've shaken off the excess energy, find a quiet place where you can sit and breathe for a few minutes.

Inhaling and exhaling from deep in your belly, remind yourself how much you've prepared for this gig. Remind yourself how much you love to sing. Then turn your mind off and just allow your breath to flow evenly in and out. If any distracting thoughts or feelings invade your mind, allow them to float away. Return to your breathing. Count your breaths (inhale and exhale counts for one breath) up to ten and then backwards from ten to one.

Breathing like this for as little as five minutes before a performance will help you to center yourself and settle down.

Step 3. Calm Your Mind

Scientists have estimated that our conscious thoughts (thoughts we are aware of having) comprise less than 10 percent of what actually goes on in our minds. All the rest of our brainpower is lodged in the subconscious mind. This amazing part of the brain coordinates all the programs that keep our bodies alive. It is also the storehouse of our imagination, dreams, and memories.

Your subconscious cannot distinguish fact from fantasy and believes unquestioningly everything that it is told. Like Aladdin's genie, the subconscious mind will create whatever it believes we most want. Instead of thinking and evaluating (properties of our rational, conscious mind), the subconscious will unquestionably act in accordance with our most deeply held beliefs, whether or not they are in alignment with what we consciously believe.

Many of us have negative programs about our singing that have been living unexamined in our subconscious minds for years. Unless we make a conscious effort to erase these old belief systems and replace them with more positive images, we will continue to unwittingly sabotage our best efforts.

The good news is that since the subconscious does not know the difference between fiction and reality, and since it does whatever it is told most forcefully to do, it responds well to positive suggestions.

There are many scientifically documented cases where hypnotism has been used to help people undergo major dental surgery without anesthesia. The hypnotist is able to convince the patient's subconscious mind that the operation will be painless, and amazingly enough, the operation in fact becomes painless.

Reprogramming your subconscious mind is an effective way to eliminate the root causes of performance anxiety. Please remember, however, that the treatment of serious mental illness is an endeavor best left to trained psychoanalysts. If doing the exercise below leaves you feeling more anxious or fearful, I recommend getting professional help for your issues.

Nightly Visualization Exercise

Your subconscious mind—the source of your imagination and your dreams—is most receptive to programming when your everyday mind is less active. For this reason, the time right before you drift off to sleep is perfect for sending positive messages to your subconscious.

Just before going to sleep each night, lie in a comfortable position. Take two or three deep breaths. Allow your body and mind to completely let go. Just as you feel yourself begin to drift off, gently bring your mind back into soft focus.

Imagine yourself standing on the stage. Feel the energy from the band behind you. Imagine the audience in front of you. Picture yourself deeply calm, relaxed, and confident as the music begins. See yourself taking a deep breath and beginning to sing. Vividly see and hear yourself giving the best performance of your life!

Mentally experience all the details of the performance: what you are wearing, what the band members are wearing, the faces of the people in the audience. In your mind's ear, hear your accompaniment backing you up flawlessly. Then, as if listening to the greatest recording ever, hear yourself singing to the rapt crowd before you.

Feel your breath flowing smoothly and your voice reaching effortlessly out to the last row. Mentally sing through your entire song.

Now hear the thunderous applause. Feel the visceral roar of appreciation from your audience as they stand up to cheer your amazing performance. Take a moment to bathe yourself in their adulation as you bow again and again. . . .

Add as many details to your fantasy as possible. If there are smells or sounds that are particularly evocative for you, add them in. The important thing is to do this visualization consistently every night for at least three weeks.

Remember when you were little and your third grade teacher would catch you daydreaming? This is exactly what I am encouraging you to do. Daydream. Fantasize. Give yourself the priceless gift of picturing yourself as completely successful.

Already, I can hear your inner skeptic saying, "That New Age poppycock may work for weak-willed nincompoops, but it will never change anything for me!" Well, of course, if you really believe that, this visualization probably will not work for you. And also, of course, nothing can help you through a performance for which you are not prepared. But if you can maintain an open mind, the results that can be gained from this simple practice may surprise you.

CHAPTER 14

The Day of the Show

At last the big day has arrived! You have been preparing for weeks, getting yourself, your music, and your band together. If you've been faithfully following all the steps in this book so far, your work is virtually over.

Unless it absolutely cannot be avoided, I never rehearse the day of the show. Last minute rehearsals are often too frantic to be effective. They also tend to drain away the mental and physical energy needed for the actual performance.

Sometimes, however, the day of the show is the only practice time available. If this is your situation, it is crucial to be as organized and on point as possible. Rather than playing through all the music, talk through the material and rehearse only the most potentially troublesome areas. At all cost, avoid repeated run-throughs of entire songs (or worse yet, your whole program). If your band hasn't gotten it together by this point, it is highly unlikely that they will do so in the next couple of hours. Excessive last minute practice will only make you tired and tense.

BERKLEE VOCALISTS SHARE THEIR PRE-PERFORMANCE RITUALS

As I was writing this chapter, I asked some of my colleagues how they prepared themselves for performance.

"After stretching, I do easy vocalizing from the lower register to the top of my chest sound on an open vowel like 'ah.' I also use the vowel sound of 'ee' to help employ the resonating of the head tone. After that, I meditate and pray, asking the positive force in my life to grant me the blessing of control and oneness among my instrument's characteristics: sound, texture, emotion, honesty, presence, and overall direction."

—Armsted Christian, Associate Professor (performances with artists such as Patti Austin, Diana Ross, and Special EFX)

"Positive thinking and visualization of a great, successful performance are two very important techniques I still practice to get ready for the gig. Taking a moment or two, two or three times a day in the few days prior to a performance to meditate on these ideas helps channel my energy towards the music and the audience and away from anxiety, negative vibes, and stage fright. It is also a great way for me to rehearse in my mind the physical, emotional, and spiritual goals of the concert."

—Lisa Thorson, Jazz Vocalist, Professor (leader of the Lisa Thorson Quintet, additional performances with artists such as Sheila Jordan, Harvie Swartz, Kenny Wheeler, and Herb Pomeroy)

"Right before I go on stage, I get in a quiet space where I can come from a place of humility. To do my best I need to be in a giving place, not a diva place. Every performance, I strive to give my best, not for myself, but for the audience."

—Renese King, Gospel Artist (soloist with the Boston Pops)

"I like to build rapport with the band by having a meal together in the hours before the show. However, as hit time approaches, I choose solitude. Right before the show, I go inside, pray, and get myself in the mood."

—Diane Richardson, Ph.D, Associate Professor of Voice
(leader of Split Image)

"For me, it's always important to warm up for maybe about ten minutes. I use hums, lip trills, and arpeggios to open up the upper register. I might also sing a portion of a song or take a riff and sing it in every key, depending on the type of gig I'm doing. The other thing that is good for the spirit is a little prayer. It helps to calm the spirit and soothe the nerves."

—Gabrielle Goodman, Associate Professor (performances with Chaka Khan and Roberta Flack; recordings with Christian McBride, Terri Lyne Carrington, and Mulgrew Miller)

BACKSTAGE ATMOSPHERE

I like to spend the hour before an important show alone. In the most peaceful place I can find backstage, I take myself through the warm-up routine listed in chapter 12. If I am feeling really nervous, I'll use the calming and centering techniques in chapter 13.

This is, of course, a highly personal choice. Some folks gather energy before a performance by joking and laughing backstage with trusted friends. Others find the presence of their best friend or significant other helps to calm and steady them. The important thing is to know yourself well enough to know what setting best fits your needs.

Sometimes, other performers will try to draw you into conversation backstage. There is a lot of nervous energy flying around, and some folks like to discharge theirs by chattering away about whatever to whomever. Unless you thrive on that kind of thing, I recommend that you avoid too much interaction with other performers before the show. If you like them, make a date to hang out sometime later. But the few minutes right before you go on are irreplaceable and should be spent free from unnecessary distractions.

Another thing I try to avoid doing is watching other acts immediately before I am supposed to go on. If they sound great and the audience loves them, I might be tempted to feel insecure and wonder how my own show will be received. On the other hand, if their act bombs, I might feel even worse, imagining that their failure will soon be mine.

Right before any performance is an excellent time to remind yourself that every human being is unique. Each of us has an irreplaceable, God-given talent that belongs to no one else on this planet. Whether or not the judges, the audience, or even your friends and family like your show is ultimately beside the point.

If they like what we do, of course, we are happy. But if you are a true performer, you will get a kick from singing, whether it's alone in the shower or before a crowd of thousands. And this kick—the pure joy and exuberance that comes from doing something you love to do well—is exactly what will draw audiences to your music. The results may be out of our control, but the pure unvarnished joy of singing will always be there, regardless of the outcome.

COPING WITH THE UNEXPECTED

You've done all you possibly can to insure a good performance. But no matter how hard you plan or how thoroughly you prepare, something unexpected is bound to occur. Just call it Murphy's Law at work.

How you handle these inevitable unpredictable moments can make or break your show. These things happen to the best of us and are part of the crazy adventure of a performer's life. As long as you remain relaxed and confident, your band and your audience probably will, too.

You suddenly forget the words in the middle of a song? No problem. Just riff for a while or improvise some new ones. (When in doubt, "Oh baby" covers a multitude of sins!) Your guitar string breaks in the middle of the big solo? Fine, just finish it out as best you can on the other strings. A drastic feedback episode erupts in the middle of your tenderest ballad? From a relaxed place of confidence, you will know whether to just ignore it or make a quick segue to an instrumental selection.

After the concert, there will be plenty of time to address the problem and figure out how to avoid having it happen again. On stage, there's nothing you can do but just roll with the energy of the moment. Whatever happens, remember that your audience wants to enjoy you and enjoy your show. They will put up with a surprising number of mishaps and remain on your side as long as you seem to be enjoying yourself.

CHAPTER 15

Effective Performance: Delivering Your Song

Have you ever been to a concert where the singer gave you goose bumps? When these magic moments happen, people will say, "She sings with such heart," or "He has such charisma!" We are trying to verbalize the effect that the energy of this performance has had on us. These sensations are not easily defined. Nor can they be reliably reproduced in a laboratory. Nonetheless, eliciting these sensations from an audience is at the heart of the craft of performance.

ENERGY, POSTURE, AND BODY LANGUAGE

As a vocalist, you are in the storytelling business. Every song you sing has been written to provoke a specific response in your audience. Your job as a performer is twofold. First, you must consciously decide what kind of audience response you are looking for in each song. Then, you must polish every aspect of your performance in order to successfully evoke the desired response.

As you learned in chapter 1, the first step in this process is to study the song in detail. What is its mood? How do the lyrics and the melody create this mood? Where is the climax of the song? What parts do you need to emphasize or de-emphasize in order to sell the song's message to your audience? If you have prepared as I suggested, you should already know the answers to most of these questions.

The next step is to make your body language fully consistent with the message of your song. For example, you are singing "You Oughta Know" by Alanis Morissette. This is a *very* angry song. In order for you to be effective, you are going to have to project some serious rage out into the audience.

In the privacy of your home, practice in front of the mirror. Imagine that your lover had just disrespected you in the worst possible way. Allow yourself to really feel and be that energy. Now speak the words of the song as if you were telling the no-count slimebag exactly what you thought of them. All the time, watch yourself in the mirror. Are you convincing? Did you scare yourself?

Next, try singing the song. Usually when we practice, we pay attention to the musical elements of the song: the melody, harmony, and rhythm. This time, I want you to focus on the energy of the song only. Even if you go off key or get the rhythm wrong, keep belting it out. For the purposes of this practice, your song is a success if you can successfully capture and project the anger of the song through your body.

Here are some things to look for:

- **Posture.** If it's an angry song you're singing, your posture should be assertive, maybe even aggressive. Though you must never lose touch with your breath or tense up to the detriment of your tone production, you are trying to push your way into your audience's headspace. You want to force them to feel things from your character's point of view.

- **Facial Expressions.** How do people's faces look when they're angry? Sad? Ecstatic? Your singing will touch people far more deeply if your facial expressions are in harmony with the message of your song. When practicing in front of the mirror, pay particular attention to your eyes—"the windows of the soul." If you are really feeling your song, your eyes will tell the story and convey the desired message to your audience. As you sing, you want each member of the audience to feel that you are singing your song to them personally. You don't have to look directly at specific people in order to achieve this feeling. You can look a little bit over their heads. But be sure to shift your gaze from time to time as you perform so that the entire audience will feel included.

- **Movement.** Along with your posture, articulation, and facial expressions, your body movements should support the message of the song. For example, you don't want to sing a tender love song with your face screwed up in a horrible grimace and your hands in clenched fists at your sides. Every part of your performance should be consistent in order for it to be believed by your audience. Study yourself carefully in the mirror to eliminate nervous ticks and unconscious repetitive gestures from your performance. The goal is to make your movements onstage as clear and unequivocal as possible.

DICTION

It is crucial that our words be clearly understood by the audience. Otherwise, we might as well be babbling nonsense syllables.

Today's pop songs are sung in the vernacular. No one wants to hear you declaim every syllable of Stevie Wonder's "Superstition" in flawlessly articulated King's English. However, it is equally true that Stevie's lyrics must be made intelligible to the listener for the song to be effective. What good is a song about superstition if no one can understand what Stevie's superstitions are and how they affected his childhood? If you just mumble your way through the lyrics, the song's key message will be lost.

Our challenge as singers of today's music is to be both stylistically appropriate and clearly understood at the same time. When in doubt, my feeling is to err on the side of clarity. Unless the words of the song are absolute nonsense, they are there for a reason and should be given their due in performance.

In chapter 5, I have given some tips on how to practice memorizing your lyrics. I would also recommend practicing speaking your words in front of the mirror. Do you convince yourself? Your audience should feel that you are talking to each of them as an individual, telling them an utterly fascinating story. You want them to be sitting on the edge of their seats waiting breathlessly for your next word.

APPEARANCE

Your appearance onstage is the very first thing that the audience vibes on, before you have even sung a note.

There are as many different ways to dress onstage as there are people, and no one way is necessarily more valid than another. The key thing is to dress in the style that is comfortable for you and appropriate to the nature of the performance you are giving.

Your look will set the stage for your music and should be fully consistent with everything else about your show in order to achieve the greatest impact.

No one expects you to play a death-metal gig in a three-piece suit and tie. Similarly, for your opening night at Carnegie Hall, a formal gown or tuxedo would probably be the best choice. If you are trying to be the next glam sensation, you will want to avoid jeans and sneakers onstage. On the other hand, if you are like me—a refugee from the flower power era—that tie-dyed shirt you've been holding onto might just set the right touch at your sixties rock gig.

You get the idea. Your look is important. And your look is individual. It's up to you to choose. Just be sure it's in harmony with everything else that will take place onstage during your performance.

CHAPTER 16

After the Performance

FRIENDS, FAMILY, AND FEEDBACK: AVOIDING THE PRAISE/REJECTION TRAP

In the heat of performance, you are as free and unfettered as a child, living from note to note in the current moment. There is no high like it.

For quite some time after the show, be aware that you may still be under the sway of your inner child. You will feel open and spontaneous, but you may also feel a lot more vulnerable than usual. Since part of you feels like a little kid, it can be hard not to react like one when someone critiques your performance.

The need for approval from parents, teachers, and other authority figures plays a major role in our childhood development. We have been raised to place great weight on the opinions of others. So if your tone-deaf best friend comes backstage after the show to tell you that your second set was weak, the little kid in you will probably take him more seriously than you would if he said the same thing three days later.

For this reason, I recommend that you take any feedback you receive immediately after the show with a grain of salt. Whether people love or hate what you did, you are in no position to properly evaluate their responses until much later on.

Whenever possible, I like to have my concerts recorded. In a couple of days when I am feeling 100 percent mature, I will sit down and listen. By then, I will be able to evaluate objectively what worked and what didn't in my performance.

Learning from Your Mistakes and Moving On

Sitting in the comfort of your living room either alone or with a teacher or trusted friend, you are now ready to really do a full postmortem on your performance. Hopefully, at least a day or two has gone by and you are able to look at your work objectively. Just as it was important immediately before, during, and after the show to reserve judgment and allow your creative inner child the freedom to perform unfettered, now it is equally important to bring your analytical adult self to the table when reviewing your show.

Try to see your performance not as you felt it to be, but as someone else might see it from the audience. I often like to imagine that I am watching someone else's performance rather than my own. Pick it apart objectively. What worked? What didn't? Where did the audience applaud the most? What went over less well? How was your pitch? Your rhythm? How tight was your band? Make notes to yourself for the next time. What would you change? What would you keep? What things were beyond your control, and how did you handle them?

There is no greater teacher than experience. The most nightmarish gig can be of great benefit if you can step back from it a bit and learn from what went wrong. All great performers have had ups and downs. There is no shame in something going wrong. The only shame is in not learning from your mistakes so that you can give a better show the next time.

CHAPTER 17

Communication 101: Getting the Word Out

Your show is competing for an audience not only with all the other events in your area, but also with the TV, the Internet, and wherever else people turn to for entertainment. To get people to leave the comfort of their homes and come see you, you are going to have to launch an effective PR campaign.

Getting Started: Research Is Everything

The first step in any marketing campaign is to assess your audience. Who are they? What radio stations do they listen to? What Internet sites do they visit? Where do they hang out? How do they get news about music events in their community? The more you can know about these folks, the better, because your publicity campaign must reach out to them from every possible angle.

Next, you will want to contact all the media outlets that target your prospective audience. Develop an ongoing database containing the names and titles of all the people at each organization that are involved with reporting on live music. Internet sites, webzines, and blogs are vital tools in today's cyber world for getting the word out about your show. If your target audience is thirty or younger, the Internet will probably be a more effective publicity tool than a local newspaper or radio station. To reach this important market, consider getting a page on Facebook or MySpace to announce your upcoming show. If you have a good video clip, YouTube will put it before millions of potential viewers, free of charge.

When researching your audience, check out what sites they are likely to visit and what Internet radio or podcasts they listen to. Contact the webmaster of each site first to find out what their criteria are for submitting your promotional material.

At many larger newspapers, there are at least two music critics in addition to an editor who collect information for their weekly calendar listings. Your local radio and TV stations will also have at least two different people who should be on your contact list.

Each media outlet has its own particular format for PR submissions. In your database next to the organization's name, you will want to enter answers to the following questions:

1. How many weeks in advance must your promo be received?
2. Would they prefer you to submit it by hard copy, by e-mail, or in both formats?
3. If you are contacting music critics, would they like a copy of your latest CD, or just the address of your Web site?

Knowledge is power, so find out as much as you can.

Promo Materials

Once you have identified the folks who are going to help you publicize your event, the next step is to put together your promo package. The basic promo package consists of your picture, your bio and press clippings, your CD, and a press release announcing the specific gig you wish to publicize.

You will not need to send your full package to everyone. After you have done your research, you can check your database to see which organizations want the full package and which ones simply want an e-mail announcement and a link to your Web site.

Pictures

Your promo shot is the most important part of your press kit.

People are visual by nature, and people in the media are no exception. In order to get your picture on the front page, it must stand out from the hundreds of other pictures competing for space in the paper that day.

If you only have a small amount of money to spend on publicity, I recommend that you spend a disproportional amount of your funds on your picture. Don't skimp in this regard.

If at all possible, go to a professional photographer who has a proven track record in entertainment work. Just because your sister has a nice camera and loves music does not mean that she should do your photo shoot.

You are looking for a professional who can put you at ease during the shoot and who will capture the essence of who you are as a performer in an eye-catching manner.

Many professional photographers have packages that they offer—so many 8x10s, so many 5x7s, so many wallet-sized photos, and a JPEG on CD. With our entrance into the digital age, the requirements of many newspapers and magazines have changed. Years ago, the black and white 8x10 glossy was the industry standard. Now, many media outlets prefer either a full color JPEG or a 3x5 color print.

Your Press Release

The next important part of your promo materials is the press release announcing your gig. Writing about yourself can be surprisingly difficult. You can't be too modest, but you don't want to be too overblown either ("Zeke Smith announces the best musical show of the decade!") Remember, you are asking people to spend their precious time and money on you. Your press release must pique their interest and motivate them to come out.

A press release has a specific format that should be followed to insure the widest media exposure. At the top of the page in capital letters, put "FOR IMME-DIATE RELEASE." Next, create a one-sentence hook that describes your event in as catchy a manner as possible.

In the next paragraph, your press release should succinctly answer each of the following five questions:

- WHO is performing?
- WHAT is the performance?
- WHERE is the performance?
- WHEN is the performance?
- HOW MUCH is the performance?

Also, your press release should always contain a prominently placed contact name and phone number.

The next two or three paragraphs of your release can add more detail to the information you have already outlined. This way, if someone wishes to write an article about you, they will have enough information for either a short or a long piece, depending on the amount of space they have.

Here's a sample:

FOR IMMEDIATE RELEASE

Contact: Joe Schmo (123) 456-7890

Danny Volume and his band **The Headaches** rock for the environment in a **Valentine's Day** benefit at the **Rotgut Lounge**.

Rock out and save the world at the same time.

On **Thursday, February 14** at 8 P.M., the **Rotgut Lounge, 144 Metropolitan Avenue**, Metropolis will host local rock sensation **Danny Volume** with his group **The Headaches** in a special Valentine's Day benefit performance. Admission charge is $10 in advance, $15 at the door.

All funds from this show will be donated to the Good Doobies Environmental Fund. Tickets are available by phone 987-654-3210, or online at www.RotgutLounge.com.

Danny Volume has recently returned to the Metropolis area from a three-year stint as a background singer with the band Famous Rock Starz. Now fronting his own band, Danny and The Headaches have been performing to sold out audiences throughout the Midwest. Volume's new CD called *Chug-A-Lug That Arizona Tea* has been receiving major airplay on college stations such as KBAC and KZAZ.

Danny and his new band also received rave reviews from the critics:

"Volume really rocks!" ***Rolling Pebble***

"Volume and the Headaches are the real deal!" ***Metropolis Rag***

A native of Metropolis's gritty West Side, Volume first got his start playing for dances at Roosevelt High School before leaving the area to seek fame and fortune on the Lower East Side of New York City... etc.

Your Bio

Your bio is where the media is going to get all their background information about you. If you are interviewed on TV or radio, the host will have (hopefully) skimmed your bio to glean the relevant facts on which to base his questions.

Your bio should be short (no more than a page long) and clearly written so that whoever's interested can find your relevant facts at a glance. Although it's called a bio (short for biography), no one is really interested in most of your life details. You just want to hit them with the few key facts that distinguish you from all the other performers out there clamoring for an interview. The bio sheet should help to bring you to life, while at the same time establishing your credentials as a performing artist. Keep a clear, conversational tone that puts you before the readers in an engaging manner.

CDs and MP3s

Oddly enough, samples of your music are the least important part of your press package. When I was first getting started, I used to mail out hundreds of tapes (remember them?) to music critics and others, hoping to publicize my events. Not only did it cost me a ton of postage, but it also did not result in any meaningful press exposure. Nowadays, there is little need to mail anything, if you have samples of your music on your Web site.

Going Digital: Getting Your Web Page Together

These days, a presence on the Web is essential. A good Web page gives you a way to keep in touch with your fan base and to sell your products. Many artists have a calendar of events on their site listing when and where they will be performing. You may also want to consider having a guestbook where people can contact you to ask questions or to offer feedback about whatever.

Like everything else, though, having an effective Web site is an expenditure of time and money, so before going all out and giving your cousin Joe your life's savings to design a state-of-the-art one for you, think through exactly how much site you really need to be effective.

If you are just getting started and don't do a ton of gigs, maybe a simple two- or three-page site will suffice. MySpace.com and Facebook.com are two well-known sites that will host your page for free. Putting up a page on each of these sites will give you immediate access to millions of potential fans. As long as you can put up a picture, a bio, a list of upcoming shows, and maybe a sample of your music, you have enough to get started. When you do this, however, be sure to register your domain name (the name of your Web site), even if you are not planning to put up your own site right away. Registering your domain name (for example, mine is carolynwilkins.com) ensures that no one else can put up a site with the same name.

PEOPLE CONNECTIONS

Getting someone to personally deliver your package to a media contact increases your odds of being noticed. If you know someone who works in any capacity for a radio or TV station, don't be shy about contacting him or her for help. Media outlets in major cities receive hundreds of submissions every week from artists seeking publicity. A personal connection increases your chances of standing out from the crowd.

Because there are so many events competing for their attention, people in the media often take tips about breaking acts from music business insiders such as agents, promoters, or publicists. If you are really serious about your career and can afford it, you may want to hire your own publicist. Before signing any agreements, be sure to research this person thoroughly, and check the fine print.

You should only have to pay your publicist when they deliver tangible results (newspaper articles, TV interviews, etc.), so make sure that whoever you hire has the necessary clout to get the job done.

Your people skills are an especially valuable asset if you are just getting started in the business and don't have any media contacts. Cultivate as many people as you can. Keep a mailing list of fans and media folks, and keep in touch with them often. If you like to write, consider putting out a monthly newsletter or posting a blog about your musical activities. As you build your grassroots following, over time, you will generate a buzz that will force the media to pay attention.

If a drummer breaks a stick in the middle of a solo, he simply reaches in his stick bag and grabs another one. If a violinist accidentally crushes his Stradivarius, he may be devastated, but at least he can use his insurance money to get another violin. If you damage your voice, that's it. You're done. You may be able to continue singing, but your voice will never sound the way it did before. Never.

So please, please, *please* take care of yourself and your voice.

You have probably heard this lecture before, but sometimes in the midst of everything else, it's easy to forget. Here are some basic vocal dos and don'ts.

VOCAL HEALTH DOS AND DON'TS

Do get as much rest as possible before performances. Remember, singing is a physical activity. You wouldn't run a marathon on three hours' sleep. Neither should you do a gig in this condition.

Do drink plenty of non-carbonated water, especially before and during a performance. To sing well, it's important to keep your body hydrated. Avoid carbonated drinks and caffeine. Though they are liquids, they are not good for your vocal apparatus and can actually interfere with good tone production.

Do maintain a healthy lifestyle. Eating a balanced diet with lots of fruits and vegetables will do wonders for your energy level. So will maintaining some form of regular exercise. Remember, singing is a physical activity. When your body is rested and feeling good, you will sing better and have more energy to give to your performance.

Avoid drinking and drugging. I know these things are commonplace in the music business, but they will take a drastic toll on your voice over time. The same thing goes for smoking. These days, there is a bizarre rumor going around that being a smoker will give you the husky, smoky vocal quality so beloved of nightclub singers. This may be true, but as we all know, smoking will also give you a terminal disease guaranteed to make your last years a living hell. Is it really worth it? By working on your low range with a good teacher, it's entirely possible to develop that rich and "smoky" vocal quality without killing yourself with ciga-rettes.

One last big don't. *Don't* ignore the warning signs of vocal fatigue or illness. Often in our eagerness during the big gig, we push ourselves and our voices over the edge. If you are frequently getting hoarse for no reason, or if you get sharp pains in your throat when singing, *stop*. Pay attention, and consult with your voice teacher and your doctor immediately.

You only have one voice, so take the best care of it that you can.

PUTTING IT ALL IN PERSPECTIVE

In choosing to work on your music, you have embarked on an endlessly reward-ing life journey. Whether or not you ever break into the top 100, your music makes an enormous contribution to society. Consider, for a moment, what kind of world we would have without music. How would people articulate the depths of feeling they carry inside? Where would they turn when they needed energy and inspiration?

As creative artists, we have a responsibility to give voice to our God-given talents. After all, if you and I don't get out there and sing our songs, who will? In the struggle to express our visions, we create a ripple effect in the world around us. When others see us expanding our horizons, they in turn become inspired to work on realizing their own dreams.

Singing is good for the body, good for the mind, and good for the soul. So practice and study hard, but most of all have fun. There is no more exhilarating feeling than knowing that you are learning and growing with each new day, doing something that you love.

APPENDIX

Resources

VOCAL TECHNIQUE

Baxter, Mark. *Rock and Roll Singer's Survival Manual*. Milwaukee: Hal Leonard, 1990.

McElroy, Donna. *Vocal Practice for Performing*. DVD. Boston: Berklee Press, 2003.

Peckham, Anne. *The Contemporary Singer: Elements of Vocal Technique*. Boston: Berklee Press, 2000.

Peckham, Anne. *Singer's Handbook: A Total Vocal Workout in One Hour or Less!* Boston: Berklee Press, 2004.

Peckham, Anne. *Vocal Workouts for the Contemporary Singer*. Boston: Berklee Press, 2006.

Peckham Anne. *Vocal Technique: Developing Your Voice for Performance*. DVD. Boston: Berklee Press. 2004.

Rusch, Gloria. *The Professional Singer's Handbook*. Milwaukee: Hal Leonard, 1998.

MUSIC THEORY AND NOTATION

McGrain, Mark. *Music Notation*. Boston: Berklee Press, 1986.

Schmeling, Paul. *Berklee Music Theory Book 1*. Boston: Berklee Press, 2005.

Schmeling, Paul. *Berklee Music Theory Book 2*. Boston: Berklee Press, 2006.

Prosser, Steve. *Essential Ear Training for the Contemporary Musician*. Boston: Berklee Press, 2000.

ARRANGING AND SONGWRITING

Allen, Corey. *Arranging in the Digital World: Techniques for Arranging Popular Music Using Today's Electronic and Digital Instruments.* Boston: Berklee Press, 2000.

Baker, David. *Arranging and Composing for the Small Ensemble.* California: Alfred Publishing Company, 1983.

Callahan, Anna. *Anna's Amazing A Cappella Arranging Advice: The Collegiate A Cappella Arranging Manual.* Milwaukee: Hal Leonard, 2001.

Kachulis, Jimmy. *The Songwriter's Workshop: Harmony.* Boston: Berklee Press, 2004.

Kachulis, Jimmy. *The Songwriter's Workshop: Melody.* Boston: Berklee Press, 2005.

Pease, Ted and Pullig, Ken. *Modern Jazz Voicings: Arranging for Small and Medium Ensembles.* Boston: Berklee Press, 2001.

Stolpe, Andrea. *Popular Lyric Writing.* Boston: Berklee Press, 2007.

REHEARSAL TECHNIQUES

Beasley, Walter. *Performance Insight for Musicians.* Boston: Amenable Press, 2003.

Berklee College of Music Faculty. *The Berklee Practice Method* (11 vols, for individual instruments). Boston: Berklee Press.

Henderson, Bill. *Running Your Rock Band: Rehearsing, Financing, Touring, Succeeding.* New York: Schirmer Books, 1996.

AUDITION AND PERFORMANCE SKILLS

Green, Barry. *The Inner Game of Music.* New York: Doubleday, 1986.

Greene, Don. *Performance Success: Performing Your Best Under Pressure.* New York: Routledge Press, 2002.

Legge, Anthony. *The Art of Auditioning: A Handbook for Singers, Accompanists, and Coaches.* Peters, 2001.

Ostwald, David. F. *Acting for Singers: Creating Believable Singing Characters.* Oxford: Oxford University Press, 2005.

Salmon, Paul. *Notes for the Green Room: Coping with Stress and Anxiety in Musical Performance.* Hoboken, NJ: Jossey-Bass, 1998.

Werner, Kenny. *Effortless Mastery.* Indiana: Aebersold Press, 1996.

MUSIC BUSINESS

Baker, Bob. *Guerrilla Music Marketing Handbook.* St. Louis: Spotlight Publications, 2005.

Fisher, Jeffrey. *Ruthless Self-Promotion in the Music Industry.* Milwaukee: Hal Leonard, 1999.

Spellman, Peter. *The Self-Promoting Musician.* Boston: Berklee Press, 2000 and 2008.

SELF-CARE

Blumenfeld, Larry. *The Big Book of Relaxation: Simple Techniques to Control the Excess Stress in Your Life.* Roslyn, NY: Relaxation Co., 1994.

Cohen, Kenneth. *The Way of Qigong.* New York: Ballantine Books, 1997.

Ristad, Eloise. *A Soprano on Her Head.* Boulder: Real People Press, 1981.

WEB SITES

Musictheory.net. This site is full of basic music theory info, including some free online lessons.

Berkleemusic.com. Berklee's online school offers courses in music theory, ear training, arranging, keyboards, guitar, bass, songwriting, and more.

Voicelesson.com. New York voice teacher Mark Baxter has written several excellent books on singing and has tons of useful information and links on his site.

Jpfolks.com. Just Plain Folks is a wonderful network of over 4,000 musicians, independent record companies, and producers. Their site is full of useful articles on every aspect of the music business.

Mbsolutions.com. Music business expert Peter Spellman has a directory of music business resources on his site as well as several links and articles.

About Carolyn Wilkins

Vocalist and keyboardist Carolyn Wilkins has been an active participant in the Boston music scene as a performer, educator, and composer since 1986. Carolyn's performance experience includes radio and television appearances with her group SpiritJazz, a concert tour of South America as a Jazz Ambassador for the U.S. State Department, working as a percussionist with the Pittsburgh Symphony under Andre Previn, and playing for shows featuring Melba Moore, Nancy Wilson, and the Fifth Dimension. Carolyn has performed at Boston's Regattabar, Scullers' Grille, the Globe Jazz Festival, and the Many Colors of a Woman Jazz Festival. She has appeared in concert at Harvard, Brandeis, and Boston Universities, and has also been featured four times as a part of Boston's annual First Night Celebration.

Carolyn has released four critically acclaimed CDs of her original compositions entitled *SpiritJazz I*, *SpiritJazz II*, *Healin' Time*, and *Praise Song* on Tiphareth Records. A swinging pianist/vocalist in the tradition of Diana Krall, Shirley Horne, and Nina Simone, Carolyn's fresh and memorable songs treat subjects as diverse as sex, satire, and spirituality with warmth and humor.

A graduate of Oberlin Conservatory, Carolyn received her master's degree from Eastman School of Music. Currently a professor at Berklee College of Music, Carolyn has taught performance skills to aspiring vocalists since 1989. For more information on Carolyn Wilkins, visit her Web site at www.carolynwilkins.com.

INDEX

More Fine Publications from Berklee Press

GUITAR

BERKLEE BASIC GUITAR
by William Leavitt
Phase 1
50449460 Book Only $9.95
Phase 2
50449470 Book Only $9.95

CLASSICAL STUDIES FOR PICK-STYLE GUITAR
by William Leavitt
50449440 Book $9.95

A MODERN METHOD FOR GUITAR
by William Leavitt
Volume 1: Beginner
50449404 Book/CD $22.95
50449400 Book Only $14.95
Volume 2: Intermediate
50449410 Book Only $14.95
Volume 3: Advanced
50449420 Book $16.95

A MODERN METHOD FOR GUITAR 123 COMPLETE
by William Leavitt
50449468 Book $34.95

MELODIC RHYTHMS FOR GUITAR
by William Leavitt
50449450 Book $14.95

JAZZ IMPROVISATION FOR GUITAR
by Garrison Fewell
50449503 ....$24.95

PLAYING THE CHANGES: GUITAR
By Mitch Seidman
50449509 ....$19.95

VOICE LEADING FOR GUITAR
by John Thomas
50449498 ....$24.95

JIM KELLY GUITAR WORKSHOP SERIES

JIM KELLY'S GUITAR WORKSHOP
00695230 Book/CD $19.95
00320168 DVD/booklet $19.95

MORE GUITAR WORKSHOP
by Jim Kelly
00695306 Book/CD $14.95
00320168 DVD/booklet $19.95

BASS

CHORD STUDIES FOR ELECTRIC BASS
by Rich Appleman
50449750 Book $14.95

INSTANT BASS
by Danny Morris
50449502 Book/CD $14.95

READING CONTEMPORARY ELECTRIC BASS
by Rich Appleman
50449770 Book $19.95

ROCK BASS LINES
by Joe Santerre
50449478 Book/CD $19.95

DRUM SET

BEYOND THE BACKBEAT
by Larry Finn
50449447 Book/CD $19.95

DRUM SET WARM-UPS
by Rod Morgenstein
50449465 Book $12.95

MASTERING THE ART OF BRUSHES
by John Hazilla
50449459 Book/CD $19.95

THE READING DRUMMER
by Dave Vose
50449458 Book $9.95

SAXOPHONE

CREATIVE READING STUDIES FOR SAXOPHONE
by Joseph Viola
50449870 Book $14.95

TECHNIQUE OF THE SAXOPHONE
by Joseph Viola
50449820 Volume 1: Scale Studies $19.95
50449830 Volume 2: Chord Studies $19.95
50449840 Volume 3: Rhythm Studies $19.95

Berklee Press Publications feature material developed at the Berklee College of Music.
To browse the Berklee Press Catalog, go to www.berkleepress.com

0706

Create.
learn music online